FEAR NO EVIL ?

Books by
Steve Russo
FROM BETHANY HOUSE PUBLISHERS

Fear No Evil?

Protecting Your Teen From Today's Witchcraft

What's the Deal With Wicca?

Wildcats in the House (with Gabi Russo)

Fear No Evil?

STEVE RUSSO

BETHANY HOUSE PUBLISHERS

Minneapolis, Minnesota

Published by Bethany House Publishers
11400 Hampshire Avenue South
Bloomington, Minnesota 55438

Bethany House Publishers is a division of
Baker Publishing Group, Grand Rapids, Michigan.

Printed in the United States of America

ISBN-13: 978-0-7642-0455-5
ISBN-10: 0-7642-0455-6

Library of Congress Cataloging-in-Publication Data

Russo, Steve, 1953-
    Fear no evil? : shining God's light on the forces of darkness / Steve Russo.
        p.   cm.
    Summary: "Explores teens' interest in the supernatural—such as Wicca, the occult, Satanism, and more—and equips readers with the biblical tools needed to withstand the influences of evil"—Provided by publisher.
    Includes bibliographical references.
    ISBN-13: 978-0-7642-0455-5 (pbk. : alk. paper)
    ISBN-10: 0-7642-0455-6 (pbk. : alk. paper)
    1. Teenagers—Religious life.   2. Teenagers—Conduct of life.   3. Good and evil—Religious aspects—Christianity.   I. Title.
    BV4447.R87   2007
    261.5'13—dc22   2007023970

Dedicated to the many students I've met who
have experienced the deception of the darkness,
but through Jesus have been able
to stand up against the devil.

STEVE RUSSO is an internationally known communicator and the author of fourteen books and numerous magazine articles. He is a television personality and is the host of the syndicated daily radio feature *Real Answers,* and he was co-host of Focus on the Family's weekly teen talk show, *Life on the Edge . . . Live!* Steve is a professional drummer and a member of the Recording Academy. He makes his home in Southern California.

contents

PART ONE

WHAT YOU'RE UP AGAINST

CHAPTER 1

SATAN'S TARGETS

Dan and his buddies from school spent many late nights tapped into an obscure world of Internet chat rooms, message boards, and portals. They were especially hooked on two sites: "Letters to the Devil" and "Devil in Blighty." Sometimes they'd just hang out, listening to Radio Free Satan. In his room, above his computer, Dan had painted a white pentagram on a stereo speaker. He also started using the names "Sid" and "Master Lucifer" in chat rooms.

Dan and his friends gradually began experimenting with some satanic rituals, performing eerie ceremonies at midnight involving burning strands of their hair and fingernails. Dan started flunking out of school and, according to his teachers, developed a serious attention disorder.

† † †

Fourteen-year-old Kim had an unreasonable fear of fire and cone-shaped objects. She also struggled with night terrors of hideous robed creatures with braided hair sitting on the edge of her bed. But the worst thing of all was trying to ignore the voices in her head. They just kept bugging her with crazy and bizarre thoughts.

† † †

Nathan was sixteen when his friends gave him a copy of Anton LaVey's *Satanic Bible*, a book that spells out the doctrine of Satanism. Nathan's mind was like a dry sponge, immediately soaking up what he was reading. Up to this point, he'd been insecure and searching for something outside himself that would make him feel special. He liked the new attitude that the book gave him. Now he felt above people he used to be afraid to talk to. After all, he was a Satanist. The others believed only in God.

† † †

When Lisa was in junior high her adoptive parents kicked her out of the house. She lived on the streets for about a year and then decided to go to the West Coast to start a new life.

In Hollywood she met some people who invited her to a birthday party, where she was introduced to twenty-two-year-old Brad. That night Lisa learned that a spirit, claiming to be an old merchant seaman from five centuries ago, possessed him.

This spirit suddenly spoke directly to Lisa in a voice she thought sounded familiar—a voice she believed belonged to her father from a past life. Lisa believed that five hundred years ago, at the age of eleven, she had been brutally raped and murdered while her father was on one of his many voyages to a far-off land. This father was the merchant seaman now possessing Brad. She and her father never had a chance to say good-bye, so it was a great surprise for her to talk with him once again after all these centuries. And now whenever she wants to speak to her "daddy," she just calls Brad, who enters a trance so she can talk to him.

Today, at age sixteen, Lisa is a Wiccan witch-in-training. After searching for truth and spiritual meaning for a long time, she thinks she may have finally found the answer.

† † †

Bob put his faith and trust in Jesus at an early age and was very involved in his church youth group. He went to every Sunday morning and Wednesday night service, summer and winter camps, plus most other youth activities.

But Bob was bored. He was bored with school, church, and life in general. He started playing Dungeons & Dragons online, but he quickly became bored with the standard game. So he came up with his own version. Bob began developing a hunger for evil and violence, but he couldn't get enough online or from television, movies, or the DVDs he rented. He hungered for more—the more violent, the better. His appetite was so intense that he started reading books just because he could make the pictures so much more violent and colorful in his imagination.

Bob's cousin invited him to a party, where he smoked up for the first time. He was hooked and started going every weekend. Bob gradually progressed from marijuana to crack cocaine.

One weekend, an older college student who'd been hanging around the parties invited Bob to a "special party." Bob hesitated at first, but finally agreed to go. The party took place outside the city limits in the basement of a large house deep in the middle of an orchard.

Bob had never experienced such a party. Every kind of booze and illegal drug imaginable was there—and free. Bob immediately involved himself in every part of the party—including the special activities in a room painted with a red goat's head on the wall and a pentagram in the middle of the floor. Chanting strange-sounding songs, speaking with an evil spirit, and seeing nearly immediate results gave Bob access to an evil power he'd not experienced before.

Bob began making a weekly journey to the isolated house for the "special party." The pattern of the party was always the same. This continued for several months, and Bob began to sense the presence of a new power in his life. But this power scared him.

† † †

Five students—each with a different story and starting point. Every one somehow involved with the supernatural powers of darkness. For some it was a game. For others it was a way of escape. And others saw it as a means to get the power needed to change their situation in life.

Some of your friends may think this "Satan stuff" is all a big joke. Others may think it's cool to worship the devil.

What about you? Do you believe the devil is for real? Are you clued in that there's a spiritual battle raging all around you?

If you want answers, check out God's Word. The Bible describes the reality of spiritual warfare in Ephesians 6:12: "For we are not fighting against flesh-and-blood enemies, but against evil rulers and authorities of the unseen world, against mighty powers in this dark world, and against evil spirits in the heavenly places."

There is evidence all around us today of this massive spiritual battle. Just look at what is taking place on your campus, in the news, or in the broken families in your neighborhood. The devil is for real, he's our enemy, and he's playing for keeps. He and his troops are viciously attacking the kingdom of God. There will be no cease-fire or temporary truce.

GET A CLUE: THE BATTLE IS REAL

Even though our struggle is not against flesh and blood, the Enemy still uses people and organizations. Satan has two great allies: the world system and the flesh. Spiritual warfare involves simultaneous action on all battlefronts.

Satan's first ally is the world in which we live. Scripture tells us that the entire world is under the control of Satan (2 Corinthians 4:4; Ephesians 2:2). In this position of power, Satan uses many things of the world to lure us into a hostile position toward God. He makes sure we are bombarded by materialism, sex, and an entire philosophy of life that is opposite to everything God says. Yet those who follow Jesus are warned not to love the world or anything in the world (1 John 2:15).

The other ally of the Enemy is the sinful nature or "the flesh." Basically the flesh is our fallen humanity. When God created human beings, He made them perfect. But when the man and woman—Adam and Eve—chose to disobey God, consequences were passed down from that point on, generation to generation. Those consequences include our desires to do things and provide for our needs apart from God. Self becomes the ruler of us—not God, evidenced by adopting attitudes of craving physical pleasure, craving everything we see, and pride in our achievements and possessions (1 John 2:16).

"Craving physical pleasure" is the preoccupation with gratifying physical passions and desires. A great example of this today is our society's incredible overemphasis on sex. Have you noticed how advertisers use sex to sell everything from cars to vitamins? Everywhere we turn we're bombarded with sexually explicit messages on TV, in movies, online, and in music.

Of course, the physical passions aren't always sexual. They can also be an out-of-control desire for food, or a self-sufficient attitude that says, "I don't need God to satisfy my cravings."

The "craving for everything we see" is the unchecked desire to accumulate things. We live in a society that's consumed with "bling." Advertisers tell us we deserve to have their product or way of life, or we should get all we can get now because we're not here for a long time—just a good time. How about the new-car commercials or the ads for the hottest fashions? They're guaranteed to make you feel that what you currently own isn't quite good enough. While there's nothing wrong with admiring nice things, it becomes a problem when it goes from appreciation to a must-have mentality.

The "pride in our achievements and possessions" is being obsessed with your status or importance. Finding your identity in what you do on the football field or how well you sing or even who your family is can be a trap. Isn't it amazing how far people will go to feel important or to gain status?

Let's face it: We all struggle with the desire to serve and please ourselves, to try to live our lives ignoring God (Romans 8:5, 8; Ephesians 2:3). This tendency is still with us even after we become followers of Christ. If we're not careful, these desires can dull us to spiritual things. And remember, you're not alone in these struggles. When the devil tempted Jesus in the wilderness, these were also the areas of attack (Matthew 4:1–11).

Satan may not be directly involved when you are tempted to sin or enticed by the darkness, but he's definitely the inspiration behind it. He has constructed a massive web of evil to lure you away from God. Don't forget, you have the freedom to choose, so choose wisely, seeking advice from God at every turn.

But don't get caught in a trap of the extremes some people have: blaming the devil for everything, and seeing demons everywhere. The result is paranoia about the entire demonic world.

An equally dangerous extreme is not believing that Satan exists. If Satan can get you to believe a lie—like he doesn't exist—then he's able to do what he pleases, and you'll never blame him, fight him, or keep your guard up, watching for his subtle methods.

You may have no clue that there's a silent spiritual battle going on all around you, but that doesn't mean the battle doesn't exist. Be on the alert! Satan's up to no good, and he will do everything in his power to defeat God's plan for your life—even if you don't believe the devil is real.

DECIDE WHAT YOU'RE GOING TO DO

Once you begin to get the picture about the spiritual battle, you must decide what you're going to do. How are you going to live in the world and stay true to God, choosing His ways rather than giving in to temptation to do things the Enemy's way? And what does it mean to resist the devil?

The battle is real, and we're all involved, like it or not. You're either following Jesus or following Satan as the Commander-in-Chief of your life. There's no in-between (John 8:44; Ephesians 2:2; 1 John 3:8, 5:19). Whose side are you fighting on? You can't remain neutral. You must decide which kingdom you will stand for: light or darkness, right or wrong, heaven or hell, God or Satan.

I'm convinced that teens are the number one target of Satan. Does that surprise you? Scare you? I'm hoping it will motivate and challenge you to seriously consider what we'll be talking about in this book.

Satan already knows what the church needs to be aware of: Teens are not just the future of this nation and the world—they're the present as well. And today, more than ever, I believe God is looking for students who are serious about making a difference.

You may just be dabbling with Satanism and the occult. You may be looking for truth about what you're hearing around school or in the media. Or you may be looking to strengthen your life to stand firm with God against the Enemy. Whatever your situation, this book is for you. We'll be looking at the battle for your mind, Wicca and witchcraft, why evil is so fascinating, how to be a candle in the dark, and much more. And most important of all, you'll find some practical hands-on solutions to help you take a stand against the forces of darkness in the spiritual battle.

Study these pages carefully and apply what you learn. God wants you to be a beacon of light in your home, on your campus, and in your community. Let's prepare for battle!

THINK ABOUT IT

1. Have you or someone you know ever been involved in the occult or Satanism? How did you or this person get hooked? What was the attraction?
2. What specific evidence indicates that the spiritual battle's a reality in your own life? Do you see it in your family? On your campus? In your neighborhood? Community?
3. What is the greatest area of temptation you're struggling with? Have you given in to this temptation? If so, consider the following steps to get back on track with God:

Confess or agree with God about your sin. Read 1 John 1:9.

Turn away from that sin and back to God. Change the direction of your life. Read Proverbs 28:13.

Accept God's forgiveness. Sometimes this is the hardest thing to do. Remember, God's forgiveness is total and complete. God erases the hard drive of our life. Read Psalm 32:5.

CHAPTER 2

THE FASCINATION WITH EVIL

Allison got more than she bargained for when she followed the crowd at her high school. "Witchcraft and the occult are cool," her friends told her. Together they experimented with casting spells and many other things that had an evil slant. But it was okay, her friends told her. They were only playing games. Evil is just a state of mind. It wasn't hurting anybody. The more Allison and her friends dabbled in evil, the more she craved it.

One sleepless night she got up to grab a midnight snack. As she walked down the hallway toward the kitchen, she noticed a strange bright light in front of the refrigerator. Frightened, she heard a strange voice say to her, "Come into the light."

Fascinated by what she was seeing and hearing, Allison stepped into the light. Once inside, she saw two hallways in front of her—one was black and white, the other green and red. Then she heard the voice again, only this time it was mocking her and laughing. Allison began running through the colored hallways, frantically looking for a way out. She kept taking wrong turns as she ran, going deeper and deeper into an endless maze of passageways.

Desperate to find a way of escape, she suddenly felt the need to pray. Dropping to her knees, she cried out to God for help. When she was done praying and opened her eyes, Allison found herself back in the kitchen.

Later that week she met a guy at school named Nathan, and she shared her experience with him. Nathan suggested that Allison talk to his pastor about it. When they got together, Nathan's pastor spoke with Allison about the dangers of playing around with evil—even though what she'd been doing seemed so innocent. He went on to explain that anything evil or wicked is offensive to God and harms those involved. Allison began to realize that if she kept dabbling with the darkness, it would cause only more problems in her life.

Was Allison's experience a bad dream, or did it really happen? Only God knows for sure. But if you were to ask Allison, she would say that it was very real to her, real enough to get her attention and motivate her to make some changes in her life.

In the last few years there's been a tremendous increase in the preoccupation with evil and the occult throughout the world. Many teens today are like Allison—they're fascinated with evil things. They want to dabble and see what will happen if they do something wicked. It's like they're trying to see how close they can get to the fire without actually getting burned.

Some are enticed to play with evil because they're interested in forces and power greater than themselves. They're looking for help to deal with the difficult issues of life. Others find evil interesting and appealing because they're bored. Their lives lack meaning and purpose. They get up every day and go through the same routine with no goals or direction in life. Wickedness and the things of the occult can look very appealing. This fascination quickly turns into a growing appetite and eventually an obsession with the darkness. Most of the time things evolve so gradually that these people don't even realize what they're getting into. Just like Allison, they slowly and subtly get sucked in, unaware of what's happening. No one wakes up one morning and suddenly decides to do evil, horrible things.

Perhaps evil's greatest appeal—and deception—is its appearance as fun and entertaining. Movies, TV shows, cartoons, magazines, books, music, Web sites, and games can sometimes have an element of evilness that baits and hooks our curiosity. Such entertainment can appear to be funny, crazy, or even scary.

Take *Revolver* magazine, for example. Here's a publication designed for heavy metal and hard rock fans that is supposed to communicate what's hot in music and culture. But the method they use to convey their information often includes articles, artwork, and photos that encourage rebellion, substance abuse, immorality, and occult activity. *Thrasher* magazine, designed for skaters and thrashers, uses similar methods aimed at their readers. Or consider mega-selling author J. K. Rowling's HARRY POTTER novels turned into movies, desensitizing millions of kids and adults to witchcraft.

When evil comes packaged in the form of entertainment or amusement, it disarms us to the dangers and the truth that we are playing with spiritual fire. Add this to the reality that we live in a society that doesn't believe in good and evil or right and wrong, and you have a volatile mix. Remember, whether it's Harry Potter or any other form of entertainment, take seriously God's word of warning in Ephesians 4:27 to not give the devil a foothold in your life.

THE SOURCE OF EVIL

Have you ever wondered how to know when something is evil and where evil came from? Webster's dictionary defines evil as "not good morally; arising from actual or imputed bad character or conduct; causing discomfort or repulsion; and causing harm." The Bible defines evil as being bad and harmful: bad (morally evil) in the sense that doing something evil is disobeying God, and harmful (naturally evil) because of the consequences people experience as a result of their disobedience. To do evil is to be in opposition to God, which makes it sin.

Evil came into being because of the freedom of choice. Evil was a necessary risk when God allowed people and angelic beings to have free will. He knew there was the possibility that someone would choose to rebel against Him. And that's exactly what Satan did (Ezekiel 28:15).

We don't completely understand why God allows evil, but we do know that He is able to bring glory to himself through evil by expressing the grace (God's undeserved favor and goodness) and justice that are part of His character. Check out what the Bible says in Romans 9:22–23: "Even though God has the right to show his anger and his power, he is very patient with those on whom his anger falls, who are destined for destruction. He does this to make the riches of his glory shine even brighter on those to whom he shows mercy, who were prepared in advance for glory."

God is free to act however He chooses because He is God. (He is incapable of choosing to do evil, though, since it violates His nature.) This includes dealing in patience and mercy with those who have used the freedom of choice to do evil rather than to follow Him and choose what is good and right. And even though He hates sin and must ultimately judge it, His goodness and love are constantly going out, even to those involved in rebellion and evil. By allowing evil and wickedness into our world—and the freedom to choose—God can demonstrate His awesome love and care for each one of us.

The Bible teaches that the one behind all the wickedness in the world is Satan himself—the granddaddy of evil. Second Thessalonians 3:3 calls him the "evil one." Satan began his wicked work in this world back with the very first man and woman—Adam and Eve in the garden of Eden.

While Adam and Eve were still sinless, they lived in Paradise in a perfect relationship with God. Then Satan, disguised as a serpent, tempted Eve with a lie to disobey God. She willfully chose to listen to the lie and ate the forbidden fruit. Adam followed what Eve had done, and God kicked them out of the garden of Eden as one of the consequences for their disobedience. Now they were separated from that wonderful, perfect, close relationship with God (Genesis 3). As another consequence of their rebellion against God, sin entered Adam and Eve and every human born after them.

Because of Adam and Eve's choice to disobey God, you and I inherited this spiritual, terminal disease called sin. The Bible describes sin in several different ways, including making a mistake or going off course (Ezekiel 34:5–6; Isaiah 28:7), disobedience (Romans 1:30; 2 Timothy 3:2), and missing the mark—hitting the wrong target (Proverbs 19:2; Romans 3:23). Sin can also be doing something that outwardly appears to be good, but the motivation for doing it is to gain the approval of other people rather than God (Matthew 6:2, 5, 16).

But at its very core, sin is simply failing to let God be God (ruler, controller, leader, Lord) in your life. It's replacing God with anything or anyone else in your life that belongs only to God. This happens when we believe the devil's lie that our way (or someone else's) is better than God's. Once we take our eyes off trusting God's perfect ways and wisdom, doubt creeps in and we start wondering if God is really who He claims to be and if the Bible really is true.

And though this evil spiritual disease is worse than cancer or AIDS, having the potential to claim everyone's life, there is a cure. Romans 5:8 says, "But God showed his great love for us by sending Christ to die for us while we were still sinners." The antidote for sin is found in a personal relationship with Jesus. That's the good news.

THE STRUGGLE

In the previous chapter I mentioned that spiritual warfare involves more than just Satan and his demonic forces of darkness. It also includes our battle with the world system and our sin nature—our rebellious self that's dominated by sin and is in opposition to God. The devil's evil influence can be seen on both of these battlefronts.

The things of the world won't last. We are told not to love these things because they are not from God. And if the weaknesses of our human flesh are left unchecked, we develop patterns that can be deadly to our spiritual well-being. God values self-control (not the craving for physical pleasure), a spirit of generosity (not the craving for everything we see), and humble service (not boasting about our achievements and possessions). When Satan attacks you with these temptations, focus instead on satisfaction and where it comes from. Learn not only to say no but also to be fulfilled with who you are and what you have.

Check out what the Bible says:

> I have learned how to be content with whatever I have. I know how to live on almost nothing or with everything. I have learned the secret of living in every situation, whether it is with a full stomach or empty, with plenty or little. For I can do everything through Christ, who gives me strength. (Philippians 4:11–13)

The key is to trust God and depend on Him for direction and satisfaction in every dimension of your life. But sometimes it's easy to think that you have it pretty well together and you don't need to consult God in a certain area of your life. I wish I could say I've never been caught in that trap, but I have. Maybe you can relate.

A close call

I was a new Christian and was convinced that God wanted to use me to win one of my former high school sweethearts to Christ. After several years without contact, she had sent me a note suggesting that we get together during the Christmas holidays. *This is it,* I thought. *We can get back together and fall in love. She'll give her life to Jesus, and we'll live happily ever after.*

There was just one problem with my plan. I was leaving God totally out of the picture. I had decided that I could handle this one on my own. I thought God had other more important things to deal with—like running the universe. Some friends in the college group at the church I attended repeatedly warned me about the dangers of ignoring God's desires for this area of my life. They told me to consider what the Bible said concerning dating non-Christians. They felt my motive in wanting my ex-girlfriend to come to Christ was good, but they cautioned me that oftentimes it is easier for a Christian to get pulled down into a compromising situation than for him to pull the non-Christian up—especially in a dating situation.

On the first night back together everything started out great, until we went to dinner. In the restaurant I noticed that she had developed some habits I wasn't crazy about. She invited me to participate. I began to rationalize the need to make her feel comfortable, so I concluded that a little bit wouldn't hurt me.

Then she invited me over to her apartment to look at our old yearbooks and pictures from things we'd done together, like proms. It seemed innocent enough to me, and I figured it would be a good chance to tell her about the Lord (so far He hadn't fit comfortably into our conversation). Once at her place, she began to close all the drapes and said she wanted to change into something more comfortable to "give me a night I would never forget."

All of a sudden it was as if someone grabbed me by the shirt and picked me up. I told her I had to go, then I walked out the door and drove away. I never saw her again. When I look back on the situation, I realize God spared me the pain of compromise and disobedience to the standards of His Word. I was very fortunate that He rescued me from giving in to the temptation that Satan had attacked me with. Who knows what the consequences might have been for leaving God out of this dimension of my life. The results could have been disastrous.

As I have grown in my relationship with Jesus, I have come to realize that God wants to be part of every area of my life, no matter how small and insignificant I might think it is. I've learned the importance of having a biblical worldview—a filter I look at life through—to make positive choices and consider the consequences of my decisions. And I've also learned that the devil will often tempt us with things that look good but are designed to sidetrack us and keep us from experiencing God's best.

If we are to respond to God in the way He desires and live the quality of life that He has designed for us, we've got to stop acting based on motives that reflect the world's value system. Make sure to check the loyalty of your heart and the focus of your mind. And as you do this, follow the advice in 1 Thessalonians 5:22: "Stay away from every kind of evil."

Be alert. Satan is up to no good. He will do everything in his power to defeat God's will for you. And he doesn't approach everyone in the same way. He designs a subtle way of attack for each person based on their weakness or when they're not paying attention. What is temptation for one person may or may not be a problem for someone else.

THE SEARCH FOR POWER

For a guy named Mark David Chapman, the devil's attack was unique and subtle. His fascination with evil revolved around his search for power, which eventually became an opening for Satan's influence. And it had devastating results.

It was the early 1960s, when the Beatles' popularity exploded in America. Mark Chapman's family lived in Decatur, Georgia, where his father gave Mark his first rock 'n' roll album, *Meet the Beatles*. Like millions of fans in America, nine-year-old Mark immediately fell under the spell of Beatlemania and would be influenced dramatically by the group's music until he was an adult.

Mark was a very lonely child who would often escape into a world of imaginary people. According to Chapman, hundreds of thousands of them lived in the walls of his bedroom, and he was their king. It was his way of coping with an abusive father.

When Mark was fourteen, the Beatles released *Magical Mystery Tour*, an album filled with drug-inspired imagery. Mark eagerly entered into the world of LSD until finding a direction for his life, several years later, working with refugees as a YMCA camp counselor. Everyone thought he was terrific, including his staff of fifteen.

When the camp closed down, he decided to go to college. He went from being a "big man at camp" to a "nobody on campus," the same kind of nobody he'd been when he was a little kid. Severe depression took over Mark's life. He dropped out of college and bought a one-way ticket to Hawaii to kill himself.

His attempt failed and after a few weeks in the hospital he was released, got a job, and met a travel agent named Gloria. He and Gloria fell in love and were married, but the honeymoon was quickly over as Gloria watched this quiet, gentle man turn into a violent, unpredictable stranger. When Mark got frustrated he would grab his wife and hit her, just as his father had done to his mother.

Mark seemed to be struggling to find himself. He was moody and drifted from job to job. Deep inside he was losing his grip on reality. At the same time he became obsessed with the book *The Catcher in the Rye,* the story of a teenager who leaves school on a three-day journey to find himself. After looking in various places in Manhattan, the main character of the book doesn't find anything but a bunch of phoniness.

Chapman assumed the identity of the fictional teenager in the book and became a believer in the character's campaign against phoniness. One day while visiting his only peaceful oasis, the public library, Mark came across a book about Beatle John Lennon, called *One Day at a Time.* As he looked at the pictures he began judging Lennon, especially after learning Lennon lived in a very expensive and exclusive co-op in Manhattan called The Dakota. This angered Chapman because he believed Lennon had sold out on the Beatles' earlier idealism.

In Chapman's disturbed mind, pieces were falling into place. Though he felt like a king-sized nobody, he saw John Lennon, a real somebody, as a phony. Suddenly this nobody wanted to strike down that somebody.

Chapman bought a .38 pistol and a plane ticket to New York City. When he checked out of his maintenance job for the last time, he signed out as John Lennon. He went to New York's Central Park to prepare to eliminate the "phony." In a television interview later, Chapman said that before he killed John Lennon, he turned to Satan because he knew he wouldn't have the strength to kill a man on his own. He went through what he thought was an appropriate satanic ritual during which he "asked Satan to give me the power to kill John Lennon."[1] He shot and killed John Lennon in front of The Dakota apartments on December 8, 1980. He was sentenced to twenty years to life in prison.

Mark David Chapman went searching for power to help him accomplish something that would give him a sense of significance. He claims he found it in Satan. In some ways, Chapman is no different from a lot of people today who are looking for a source of power to help them deal with the pain of life.

Power is an interesting concept. It can create a safe haven for those who are weaker (like a kindergarten teacher would do for her students); it can also lead those who need to follow. Power can give a person strength to achieve something good. Or power can center on self-desire, which creates havoc and pain in the lives of those under the control. (Think Saddam Hussein.) Power can also create chaos and corrupt someone if it is obtained from the wrong source and abused, as it was with Chapman. This kind of power is alluring because it is a means of control, authority, or influence over others when one feels completely powerless. And those who believe they have obtained evil power say it gives them a sense of significance among their friends.

The Bible speaks often about power. The power of Jesus Christ is described as supreme (Ephesians 1:19–21), unlimited (Matthew 28:18), and everlasting (1 Timothy 6:16), and it enables Him to bring everything under His control (Philippians 3:21). It's demonstrated in Jesus' rising from the dead (John 2:19–22), overcoming the world (John 16:33), overcoming Satan (Colossians 2:15), and destroying the works of Satan (1 John

3:8). It's a power that's full of love, and therefore life-giving or life-enhancing.

Satan's power is a counterfeit—a false copy of Christ's power. It's limited, temporary, and designed to lure people away from trusting God. His power is full of hate and anger, therefore life-destroying.

We live in an evil and seductive world. And the Bible says we must turn away from evil and do good (1 Peter 3:11). How do we do that? Thankfully, God has equipped us with every resource necessary to win the battles against the darkness—including access to His great power.

The key to obtaining this power is gained first by surrendering your life to Jesus Christ as your Savior and Lord. Deciding to live your life like and for Him. Then God will give you all the resources you need through His Son, the Holy Spirit, prayer, and the Bible. When we are bored, tempted, or need help and power to overcome the difficulties of life, we need to turn to these resources.

What God offers us should be our first resource, not our last resort. Practically, this means we need to put our hope and trust in what God tells us and not in what society, the media, or Satan tells us. Second Timothy 1:7 says, "For God has not given us a spirit of fear and timidity, but of power, love, and self-discipline." Imagine—the same power that raised Jesus from the grave is available to you and me to help us face the challenges of life! Isaiah 40:29–31 says, "He gives power to the weak and strength to the powerless. Even youths will become weak and tired, and young men will fall in exhaustion. But those who trust in the Lord will find new strength. They will soar high on wings like eagles. They will run and not grow weary. They will walk and not faint."

If you really want to experience victory over the darkness,

you must stop opening yourself up to every weird value and attitude that the world puts in your path, no matter how exciting or entertaining they may seem. The security, acceptance, and significance we need to succeed in life are found in Jesus, not the temporary things of this world. Stop being seduced and misled by these things—especially evil—and start becoming fascinated and consumed with the almighty, all-knowing, all-powerful God!

Think about it

1. How are you most often or easily tempted by evil? What do you need to do so you won't be so vulnerable to this evil enticement?
2. Have you ever been tempted to leave God out of a situation? What happened?
3. What insights did you gain from the story of Mark Chapman's search for power? What kind of power do you think most teenagers are looking for today?
4. How would you describe your relationship with Jesus? How do you think He would describe your relationship with Him?

CHAPTER 3

DO YOU KNOW YOUR ENEMY?

It was five-thirty the night before Thanksgiving when the phone rang at my office. Dan, a deputy and good friend, was calling from the sheriff's station. "Steve," he said, "can you give me five minutes?"

"What's up?" I asked. Dan explained that he and his partner had just picked up a fifteen-year-old girl in a convenience store; she had tried to kill herself.

"We're going to place her in protective custody at a local hospital," he said. "But you gotta talk to her. She really needs help."

Jennifer got on the phone and said she wanted to kill herself because no one cared. She'd been abandoned by her parents and had been living in foster homes most of her life. "I just can't take the loneliness and pain anymore," she said.

I tried to tell her that I cared about her and wanted to help. "No you don't," she said. "You don't even know me." Realizing our conversation was getting nowhere fast, I decided to change my tack. "Jennifer," I asked, "do you know where you'll go when you die?"

"Absolutely," she responded. "I'm going straight to hell."

"Is that really where you want to go?" I questioned.

"Yes," she said. "And I want to go there as soon as I can."

"Jennifer, there's another option—another place you can go when you die," I explained.

"Oh, I suppose you're going to tell me all about the lies of heaven," she said sarcastically.

"Who told you that heaven is a lie?" I asked.

"My god," she responded.

"Who's your god?"

"Satan," Jennifer replied. "And he'd never lie to me."

I desperately tried to give her the details about Satan's lies and how much Jesus loved her. "Call me when you get to the hospital," I pleaded. "I really do want to help you."

Her voice was ice-cold when she responded, "Is that all you have to say?"

"Just remember, Jennifer, Jesus loves you," I said. She hung up the phone, and I never heard from her again.

Jennifer is like many students today who have listened to the wrong voice and bought Satan's big lie. They may not all have tried to kill themselves, but they're at risk from the crafty seduction of the enemy's attacks.

We are all involved in a battle against powerful evil forces headed by a vicious fighter—Satan. It's a war between the kingdom of light and the kingdom of darkness. Between the kingdom of right and the kingdom of wrong. Between the kingdom of God and the kingdom of Satan. For us to be able to withstand his attacks we must understand the tactics of our enemy and depend on God's strength.

THE REALITY OF SATAN

Satan has done an incredible job of confusing us about his true identity. Plenty of movies, books, games, song lyrics, Web sites, and celebrities represent Satan in a way that's very different from reality. This kind of deception makes it way too easy to become a victim of Satan's trickery and attacks. Usually Satan is described in one of two ways. Sometimes he is pictured as a goofy little buffoon wearing a red suit with horns on top of his head, carrying a strange-looking pitchfork, and running around poking people. I see this every Halloween in our neighborhood. Little kids trick-or-treat dressed up as the devil in these red polyester suits, carrying a plastic pitchfork and running around saying, "Gotcha!"

Satan is also described in a completely opposite way: as a horrible-looking creature that's part human, part monster, and part alien, with bulging eyes, fire for breath, and the most hideously evil laugh imaginable. Slasher movies and horror flicks, some computer games, and even some CD covers and comic books are filled with these images.

Satan has used these and other ingenious pictures of himself to confuse and disarm us. It's no wonder so many people today don't take him seriously. There's no doubt that Satan's strategy is definitely working well.

In a national survey, teens were asked to respond to the statement, "Satan is not a living being but is a symbol of evil." More than half of teens (60 percent) said they agreed with the statement.[1] Satan would like nothing better than for people, especially those of us who are Christians, to be deceived into believing he doesn't exist. After all, if Satan isn't for real, we don't have to be concerned about spiritual warfare. And so we lose the battle.

The world will give us confusing information when it comes to spiritual things. That's why it's important to depend on what the Bible teaches. God's Word is the ultimate source of truth. And the Bible confirms the reality of Satan and gives us an accurate picture of his true character.

In Ezekiel 28 we learn much about Satan. Let's check out a few verses from this chapter in the Old Testament.

✦ "You were the model of perfection, full of wisdom and exquisite in beauty" (v. 12).

✦ "You were blameless in all you did from the day you were created until the day evil was found in you" (v. 15).

✦ "Your heart was filled with pride because of all your beauty. Your wisdom was corrupted by your love of splendor. So I threw you to the ground and exposed you to the curious gaze of kings" (v. 17).

Satan was the wisest, most powerful, and most beautiful creature ever made. Nothing else in all creation could compare to him. Yet he refused to accept the fact that all of his greatness came from God. As his pride grew, he made a horrible choice to rebel against God. His determination to take over God's kingdom and seize control of His power started a war he could never possibly win. His actions ultimately plunged all of creation, including you and me, into a deadly spiritual war.

Because of His awesome holiness, God could not tolerate rebellion and evil in His kingdom. God stripped Satan of his position of authority, drove him from heaven, and made a disgrace of him as He threw him to earth. Though this battle between God and Satan started in heaven, we're now caught right in the middle of it here on this planet. And because Satan hates God and is angry with Him, he also hates those of us who try to live our lives in a way that pleases the Lord. There's not a chance that the devil's going to let us remain untouched spiritually by his fierce attacks. He's going to throw everything he can in his arsenal of weapons to harass us and keep us from focusing on God.

THE CHARACTER OF SATAN

Now that we know more about Satan's true identity, it'll also be helpful to know more about his character—what he's really like.

Even though Satan was mortally wounded as a result of Jesus' death on the cross and resurrection, he still has a great deal of power even though it's limited (Colossians 2:15). He can only do what God allows him to do.

The biblical names given to Satan can give us insight into his character, his history, and even his behavior. Take a look at the names of Satan, their meaning, and some of the places in the Bible where you can find each of them used.

Name	Meaning	Chapter/Verse
Satan	Adversary/opponent	Zechariah 3:1; Matthew 4:10; Revelation 12:9; 20:2
Devil	Slanderer	Matthew 4:1; Ephesians 4:27
Evil One	Intrinsically evil	John 17:15; 1 John 5:18–19
Serpent	Craftiness	Genesis 3:1; 2 Corinthians 11:3
Ancient serpent	Deceiver in Eden	Revelation 12:9
Dragon	Fierce nature	Revelation 12:3, 7, 9
Abaddon	Destruction	Revelation 9:11
Apollyon	Destroyer	Revelation 9:11
Enemy	Opponent	1 Peter 5:8
Accuser of the brothers	Opposes believers before God	Revelation 12:10
Tempter	Entices people to sin	Matthew 4:3; 1 Thessalonians 3:5

Name	Meaning	Chapter/Verse
Prince of this world; the spirit who is now at work in those who are disobedient	Rules in world system	John 12:31; Ephesians 2:2
Beelzebub	Chief of the demons	Luke 11:15 NIV
Belial	Worthlessness/wickedness	2 Corinthians 6:15 NIV
God of this age	Controls philosophy of the world	2 Corinthians 4:4 NIV
Ruler of the kingdom of the air	Control of unbelievers	Ephesians 2:2 NIV
Father of lies	Perverts the truth	John 8:44 NIV
Murderer	Leads people to eternal death	John 8:44
Angel of light	Deceptive appearance	2 Corinthians 11:14

Satan is also described in 1 Peter 5:8 as a roaring lion, actively looking for opportunities to pounce on us. You might say that he's like a serial killer stalking his next victim. But if we have put our faith and trust in Jesus, there's no reason for us to live in constant fear of what Satan may do next. God has not made us fearful but, instead, has given us all the power and spiritual resources we need for every threat and attack of the devil (2 Timothy 1:7). Toward the end of the Bible, 1 John 4:4 reminds us that "the Spirit who lives in you is greater than the spirit who lives in the world."

It's easy to start believing Satan's lies that he's more powerful than God—especially when you see evidence in the wickedness all around us. Evil obviously has more power than mere humans do; however, the Bible reminds us that God is stronger. He's almighty and all-powerful. When Jesus rose from the dead, He stripped Satan and all the forces of darkness of their bogus power and authority over those who trust in Him.

As a created being, Satan is no match for the living God. When we have a personal relationship with Jesus, we can have victory over the attacks and temptations of the devil.

The strategies of Satan

Because Satan was formed above all other created beings in intelligence, he's a brilliant war planner and has developed some very clever strategies to use in his attacks against us. Part of his overall plan includes doubt, difficulties, self-sufficiency, false teaching, confusion, and distractions. Let's take a closer look at each one of these tactics and how we can better defend ourselves.

Doubt

Satan wants to weaken God's character and credibility. He started this back in the garden of Eden with the first man and woman. Satan wanted Adam and Eve to doubt what God had said and why He said it (Genesis 3). In turn, the devil wants us to be uncertain of who God is and what He's like. Satan would also like us to be skeptical about the promises of God's Word and even doubt that we have a relationship with Him. Satan will do all he can to trip us up through doubt.

The Bible clearly says that Satan is a liar (John 8:44) and that God is incapable of lying (Titus 1:2). When you struggle with doubt, think of examples of how God has been faithful to you in the past, and think of evidence you either know or have read about in the Bible. Keep a journal of times when God has done something in your life and reread it during times of doubt. Get your eyes off any circumstances that may be causing you to doubt and put your eyes on Jesus. Make sure you saturate your heart and mind in the Bible (Romans 10:17). If you're dealing with doubt, here are some other verses you can look at: Psalm 14:1; John 10:28; and James 1:5–8.

Difficulties

The devil will use difficulties and problems in your life to make things hard. The difficulties could include everything from stress at home with your parents to pressure at school with friends, or even different forms of persecution where you work. Satan's adversity may even come from people in your youth group at church. He tries anything and everything to frustrate God's plan for your life. Ultimately, the Enemy would like you to get so discouraged that you turn your back on God.

When the going gets tough, remember what Jesus said in John 16:33: "I have told you all this so that you may have peace in me. Here on earth you will have many trials and sorrows. But take heart, because I have overcome the world." No matter how bad things may get, Jesus promises never to leave us or turn His back on us (Hebrews 13:5). Instead of asking God why these things may be happening to you, ask Him how He wants to help you through this difficult time in your life. Here are some additional thoughts from the Bible to look at: John 15:18–20 and Romans 16:20.

Self-sufficiency

Satan wants us to trust in our own strength and resources and not rely on God. He works hard at misleading us into placing our confidence in the wrong things. This is often reinforced by the messages we hear in the world, those philosophies that are exactly opposite of what the Bible teaches, things like "The power is within you" or "It's all about you." The list goes on and on. The devil works subtly to keep us just slightly off track of where God wants us to be, making us think we can live without God.

You'll know this tactic is working when you stop connecting with God, when your prayer life becomes almost nonexistent and your time in the Bible disintegrates into basically nothing. Self-reliance is the very core of sin—living independent of God. Satan wants us to rely on ourselves and not on the resurrection power of Jesus Christ, while God wants us to rely on Him for everything. As I said earlier, God promises to provide all the help we need. The Bible teaches in John 15:5, "Apart from me you can do nothing." When you need answers or have challenges in your life to overcome, depend on God. Check out the promise in Philippians 4:13: "I can do everything through Christ, who gives me strength." How about you? Are you tempted to rely on your own strength rather than God's? Have you been trying to live your life without God? Look up Psalm 84:5 and Proverbs 3:5–6 for more help.

False teaching

The devil wants to frustrate and mislead us with wrong ideas. Have you ever noticed how many musicians on the Grammy Awards thank God for an award or dedicate their albums to God? But how many of them really know what it means to have a personal relationship with Jesus? How many of them know God as He defines himself? And what about their lifestyles and lyrics? Do they show an understanding of God?

You may have some friends at school who are members of false religions or cults (Mormons, Jehovah's Witnesses, etc.) that teach that Jesus was just a teacher or a good man. Other religious groups say that Jesus is here on earth now, leading them. Sometimes listening to this false teaching can be deadly.

Marshall Applewhite, also known as "Bo," was a self-described space-age shepherd on a mission to lead a flock of humans to a higher level of existence through his cult, "Heaven's Gate." On their Web site was this convoluted message: "The joy is that our Older Member in the Evolutionary Level Above Human (the 'Kingdom of Heaven') has made it clear to us that Hale-Bopp's approach is the 'marker' we've been waiting for—the time for the arrival of the spacecraft from the Level Above Human to take us home to 'Their World'—in the literal Heavens. Our 22 years of classroom here on planet earth is finally coming to conclusion—'graduation' from the Human Evolutionary Level."[2]

The cult members apparently believed they were going to meet a UFO hiding behind the Hale-Bopp comet by way of suicide. The Heaven's Gate Web site didn't mention suicide but promoted a "willful exit" as the road to "entering the Kingdom of Heaven."

So Applewhite and thirty-eight of his followers ended up dead in a hilltop mansion in Rancho Santa Fe, California. They all died in a carefully orchestrated suicide that took place over three days in a calm, ritualistic fashion. Although the mass suicide involved drugs, it wasn't a drug-crazed party, according to a CNN report (March 27, 1997). The drugs were ingested only for the specific purpose of taking their own lives. Prior to his or her death, each member of the organization gave a brief videotaped statement stating that "we're going to a better place." The members were described as "quite jovial and excited about moving on to the next stage."

I'm convinced that most of these people would be alive today if they had recognized the lies of the Enemy. Jesus made it very clear in John 14:6 that He is the only way to get to heaven—not hitching a ride on a spacecraft!

Or look at what's happened since the horrible events of September 11, 2001. Well-meaning people, including pastors and leaders, have been teaching that Islam and Christianity are basically the same. It's the politically correct thing to believe in a "tolerant" society. After all, what's so bad about Islam? It's a mainstream religion, just like Christianity.

Unfortunately, lots of teens are buying this deceptive tactic of Satan's. For example, here's part of an email from sixteen-year-old Amanda, who says she's a Christian.

"In Islam, people believe in one God and that Muhammad was his prophet, and that Jesus was another prophet, who didn't fulfill God's will when he was on earth. Anyway, the point is that Christians and Muslims and Jews believe in the same God (capital G), and all three beliefs are related to Abraham. I hope I don't come across negatively. I love God soooo much (still working on the whole heart) and even more amazing, He loves me!"

Nothing could be further from the truth! Muhammad and Jesus can't both be right. This is just another lie from the devil. It's one more way to trip us up and get us off course.

The big problem is that we've very subtly strayed from what the Bible teaches. In many churches today, praise and worship music occupies a more important place than the teaching of God's Word. Many Christians do not know what they believe or why they believe it. We rely more on what other people say than on what God says—the convictions of Christians rather than Christian convictions. Or we let singing praise songs replace teaching from God's Word. As individuals, we've become biblically illiterate because we're not spending nearly enough time studying the Bible, so consequently we don't know how to respond to the issues of life God's way. We're easily led astray, and we start believing—and living—Satan's lies.

In l John 4:1–3, God gives us a test we can use to know if a belief or supposed truth is from a demon or the Holy Spirit: "Dear friends, do not believe everyone who claims to speak by the Spirit. You must test them to see if the spirit they have comes from God. For there are many false prophets in the world. This is how we know if they have the Spirit of God: If a person claiming to be a prophet acknowledges that Jesus Christ came in a real body, that person has the Spirit of God. But if someone claims to be a prophet and does not acknowledge the truth about Jesus, that person is not from God. Such a person has the spirit of the Antichrist, which you heard is coming into the world and indeed is already here."

The main way God communicates to us is through His written Word—the Bible. One of the marks of growth in your spiritual life is when you turn to the Bible more frequently in your search for answers—and even more so when that's your *first* place to go for help. Don't neglect time alone in God's Word. Remember, there's no substitute for studying the Bible—not even listening to or singing praise music. We'll talk more about this later, but in the meantime, here are some other verses to study: Luke 6:47 and 2 Timothy 3:16.

Confusion

The devil is a master at twisting messages and truth to confuse us. For example, Satan has worked hard to erode society's moral standards, making purity look old-fashioned and immorality cool. "Safe sex is okay sex," "You can drink—just don't drive," "There's no such thing as absolute truth," "All religions lead to God." Satan loves for us to be so baffled about what is right and what is wrong that we compromise our faith in Christ.

And he uses words, attitudes, and belief systems that sound logical. After all, what's so wrong with "tolerance," someone might ask us. And our foundations seem to crumble under such seemingly simple questions.

God has something to say about those who twist His truth—whether it's filtered through the world system or directly from Satan himself. Read Isaiah 5:20, which says, "What sorrow for those who say that evil is good and good is evil, that dark is light and light is dark, that bitter is sweet and sweet is bitter."

It's no wonder that living in a world like ours can be dangerous to our spiritual health. But when you're feeling confused by the world's messages, just remember that God is not the author of confusion (James 3:16), but instead He's a God of order and peace (1 Corinthians 14:33). Take time to ask God for wisdom and direction for your situation. Pray, then check out God's Word for wisdom. Here are some places to get started: Isaiah 30:21 and Philippians 4:6–7.

Do you sometimes wonder if the wisdom you've received is really from God? Check it against this list in James 3:17: "But the wisdom from above is first of all pure. It is also peace loving, gentle at all times, and willing to yield to others. It is full of mercy and good deeds. It shows no favoritism and is always sincere."

Distractions

Satan likes to work subtly by frustrating us and getting us mentally confused through distractions. These aren't necessarily evil things or some horrible intrusion into our lives. For example, when I was writing this book, I got hit with all kinds of things to distract and frustrate me. First it was problems with a new laptop that I purchased, and the company that I bought it from kept wanting me to try to repair a bad hard drive rather than just replace the first one. Then someone broke a huge window in the front of our office, and the car broke down and had to be towed to the shop—all this and much more happened within just a couple of weeks. I was totally frustrated because I knew that I needed to finish writing this book, but I kept getting sidetracked from my goal.

Don't misunderstand what I'm saying. We've got to be careful that we don't blame the devil for everything that goes wrong in our lives. Sometimes we just do dumb things, or "life stuff" just happens. But we also have to remember that we're in a spiritual battle with an enemy who ultimately wants to destroy us. And at the very least, Satan wants to keep us from experiencing God's best for our lives. As we learned earlier in this chapter, Satan is our adversary, and he's extremely crafty in his strategies of warfare.

Have you ever had an experience similar to mine? There are times when we get hit by Satan's distractions. It could be sports, music, a boyfriend or girlfriend, or it could even be problems at home. And no matter what distractions the devil may use in our individual circumstances, he has one main objective for each of us—to keep us from growing in our relationship with God. The best way for him to achieve this is to keep us out of the Bible and distract us from praying. We'll talk more about this in another chapter, but in the meantime, make your time alone with God a priority each day. It really can help you better deal with the devil's distractions and stay focused. And remember to follow the advice found in Hebrews 12:2: Keep your eyes on Jesus. Study how He ran the race of life and how He never lost sight of where He was headed.

THE REALITY OF DEMONS

God's Word teaches that the spiritual battle includes not only Satan but also his demons. Without question the Bible affirms the reality of demons. Jesus confirms the existence of demons numerous times during His earthly ministry (Matthew 10:1, 12:22–28, 15:22–28; Mark 5:1–16; Luke 10:17). Every book in the New Testament (except Hebrews) mentions demons. Many passages in the Old Testament also refer to demons.

Demons are more than just figures of speech, cosmic forces, or concepts that merely exist in our minds. They are spirit beings (Ephesians 6:12). They are not present everywhere, but they are not as restricted as human beings by the normal barriers of space.

Demons possess intelligence (Mark 1:24), emotions (Luke 8:28; James 2:19), wills (Luke 8:32), and personality (Luke 8:27–30). They can also possess superhuman strength at times, like the demon-possessed man in Mark 5:1–16. Having chosen to join Satan's rebellion against God, demons continue to oppose the purposes of God in this world. They promote false religion (1 John 4:1–4; 1 Timothy 4:1–3) and the worship of idols (Leviticus 17:7; Deuteronomy 32:17; 1 Corinthians 10:20).

A DEFEATED ENEMY

Satan's identity, his various names, his cohorts, and his strategies not only affirm the reality of his existence but also reveal his many-faceted character and the aspects of his work. He is a powerful, intelligent, and clever creature. We must never underestimate our enemy or the forces of darkness. For those who don't have a relationship with Christ, he will do all he can to keep them from deciding to live their lives for and like Jesus. He doesn't care how much we go to church, youth group activities, camps, or Christian concerts—just as long as we don't surrender our lives to Jesus. Satan's plan for those who have decided to become Christians is to keep them from growing in the strength and knowledge that comes as a result of following Jesus. And he wants to keep them from telling others how they can also find forgiveness, hope, and love in a relationship with Christ.

Despite all this, the great news is ours: Jesus is our defender, and He defeated Satan when He died on the cross. Colossians 2:15 tells us that Jesus disarmed the powers and authorities, making a public spectacle of them and triumphing over them by the cross. The devil is powerless in the presence of the Son of God. Ultimately, Satan will be judged and cast into the lake of fire for eternity along with the beast and the false prophet (Revelation 20:7–10).

We're on the winning side when we have a relationship with Jesus. God has given us all the necessary resources to withstand the attacks of the Enemy, including special spiritual weaponry and equipment. Our strategy for victory is summed up in James 4:7: "So humble yourselves before God. Resist the devil, and he will flee from you." As soldiers in a spiritual war, we need to obey our Commanding Officer and follow His leadership. Then He will give us the strength to take our stand against the Enemy.

THINK ABOUT IT

1. Have you ever known anyone like Jennifer, who was deeply involved in the occult? How could you help someone like this?

2. What strategy does the devil use most often in your life? Why? What does God want you to do in this situation to achieve victory?

3. List some specific examples of confusing messages you have noticed in the media, at school, and in the world. How can you best prepare yourself to be on guard against these subtle attacks?

CHAPTER 4

THE BATTLE FOR YOUR MIND

The ride Mission: SPACE is an awesome adventure at Disney's Epcot Center in Orlando, Florida. Guests who accept the mission will engage in a one-of-a-kind astronaut experience that launches them into a simulated space adventure—from pulse-racing liftoff to the sensations of traveling through outer space on a mission to Mars. When it first opened, it was the most technologically advanced ride ever created by Disney. In association with NASA advisors, astronauts, and scientists, Walt Disney Imagineering developed Mission: SPACE as the first ride ever created to take guests straight up in simulated flight.

The setting for the attraction is several decades into the future at the International Space Training Center. As the "crew" selected for this ultimate space mission, guests head to the dispatch area and then move to the Ready Room, where they receive a history of astronaut training and are given the role they will assume during the mission—as the commander, pilot, navigator, or engineer.

Then it's on to the preflight corridor to load into the spacecraft, receive final briefings from the CapCom (capsule communicator), and buckle in for liftoff. When the countdown reaches zero, the seats begin to rumble, white clouds of exhaust start to stir as the ascent toward the sky starts, and guests are rocketed into the galaxies. Guests hear from the CapCom and are asked to perform vital tasks that will land their spacecraft safely on Mars. But there is no mission without surprises. Guests encounter unexpected twists, turns, and other challenges that test every astronaut. Quick thinking and fast reactions are needed by each guest to successfully complete the mission.

The realism of the experience adds to its uniqueness because it mixes real science and thrill. The sensations are what the astronauts actually experience, only you never leave Epcot Center—or the building where the ride is located—even though your mind has totally convinced you that you have just experienced an incredible adventure to Mars.

The mind is an amazing thing. There's no computer in the world that can match its capabilities. But just like a computer, the mind needs to have "software" installed to enable a person to function. Most of us spend at least twelve years of our lives getting an education—installing "software" into our minds at school. But we also receive data from the music we listen to, the movies and TV shows we watch, the books and magazines we read, as well as the online sites we visit and the games we play. All the things we store in our minds are eventually going to make their way out in the things we do and say. What goes in is going to influence what comes out in the way we think, live, and behave.

For example, think about the commercials you see on TV. You've assumed your favorite couch potato position and are watching your favorite show. Then it happens—the music starts playing and you hear the words *baby-back ribs*. Your mouth begins to water and you can almost smell Chili's baby-back ribs. Your mind sends a signal to your stomach that you gotta have ribs—NOW! It doesn't matter that you stuffed your face twenty minutes ago. You're suddenly motivated to do something based on what you have seen on the screen. That's what advertising is designed to do.

WHERE IT ALL STARTS

It begins with what goes in through your eyes and ears. Once you let something into your mind, that information begins to shape your thoughts. Your thoughts then begin to form your attitudes—how you feel about someone or something. Ultimately your attitudes determine your behavior. Do you see the progression?

Have you ever wondered why you do some of the things you do? Maybe you need to take a look at the food you're feeding your mind. The Bible explains it this way: "The words you speak come from the heart—that's what defiles you. For from the heart come evil thoughts, murder, adultery, all sexual immorality, theft, lying, and slander" (Matthew 15:19). The word *heart* stands for a person's entire mental and moral activity. In other words, it describes our inner personal life—our mind and emotions. Because sin takes a seat in the center of our inner life, it can short-circuit our actions.

If a commercial can motivate us to buy something, is it possible that something we see in a movie, read in a book or online, or download to an iPod could influence our thinking in such a way as to cause us to do something—good or bad? If a sixty-second Hallmark commercial can encourage us to be kind and buy a card for someone we love, can a brutal two-hour movie subliminally encourage us to do something that's violent and harmful to others or ourselves? Think about it.

Nineteen-year-old Mark Branch killed himself after stabbing an eighteen-year-old female college student to death. When the cops searched his room, they found ninety horror movies as well as a machete and a goalie mask like those used by Jason, the grisly star of the *Friday the 13th* movies.[1]

Or what about the nine-year-old boy who sprayed a Bronx office building with gunfire? The boy explained to an astonished police sergeant how he learned to load his Uzi-style gun: "I watch a lot of TV."[2]

Obviously, these are extreme cases, and other things need to be considered in each situation, but you can't deny at least some connection with violence in the media and its effect on the mind. Researchers in all areas of the social sciences have studied the question of whether TV and other forms of media entertainment cause violence. The results have been incredibly conclusive, and numerous groups over the years have called for curbing violence in these media. Under pressure of these groups, computer game manufacturers have started to put warning labels on packaging.

And what about entertainment as a factor in other problems challenging teens today, like drug and alcohol abuse, premarital sex, or suicide? While there are many contributing factors to these problems, including the breakdown of the family, if you look carefully, you will see a direct connection between the increase in these problems and the change in our entertainment values in the last thirty years.

Satan always attacks us where we are most vulnerable: in our minds. Don't ever forget that the heat of the spiritual battle is taking place between your ears. Temptations begin in your thoughts. Ultimately that's where the war is going to be won or lost. The Bible says much about the mind. One of the key principles that we see repeated is that whatever you think about is going to be reflected in your actions. Our minds are constantly recording, storing, and processing information put in front of our eyes or into our ears. That's why it's critical to learn to filter that information. (We'll talk more about how to do this in chapter 10, "Take Control.")

The apostle Paul wrote that before we were Christians, we were separated from God and were enemies in our minds because of our evil behavior (Colossians 1:21 NIV). Without Christ, our minds can be controlled by all kinds of evil thoughts. In 2 Corinthians 4:4 we read that the god of this world, Satan, has blocked the minds of unbelievers so they cannot see the light nor hear the truth of the Gospel. In other words, when the message of God's love is presented, the devil conceals it from an unbeliever's mind. However, the Holy Spirit of God is not powerless and can break through these tactics of the Enemy.

After we become followers of Jesus, the Bible warns us not to be deceived by the craftiness of the devil, who wants to lead our minds away from sincere and pure devotion to Christ (2 Corinthians 11:3). How can the Enemy hope to accomplish this? By influencing our thinking through manipulating what we put into our minds.

What are you filling your mind with? It's amazing what's available. Be careful what you feed your mind—it may be hazardous to your spiritual and physical health.

WHOM ARE WE FiGHTiNG?

This battle raging to control and influence our thinking is coming from the same three major sources we looked at briefly in "Satan's Targets" (chapter 1).

The sinful nature

We are all born with a desire to live independent of God. This desire comes from our sin nature. This nature has been passed down through the generations from Adam and Eve to every single person except Jesus. We were born to sin, to ignore God (Romans 6:6, 17). But the power that sin has over each one of us is broken and we're set free when we put our faith and trust in Jesus (Romans 6:18). Even though the power of sin over us is broken, however, our sinful nature is still tempted by the forces of darkness and the philosophies of society and the world system.

The sinful nature is the most influential enemy facing the

Christian (Romans 8:1–17; Galatians 3:3; Ephesians 2:3). It's what gives our other two enemies, the world and the devil, the chance to operate effectively in our minds.

The world

This enemy is not the physical planet we live on, but rather the society that we live in that influences our way of thinking. Many times in the New Testament, the world is presented as something hostile to God (John 17:14, 18:36; 1 Corinthians 3:19; 1 John 2:15–17). The world's empty ideas and philosophies that influence thinking are different in every country and change with every generation. At the heart of this kind of thinking is a continual stirring up of our sinful nature to indulge in a variety of wrong and evil behaviors. And often this worldliness is presented in an appealing way. Despite the pull of society's thoughts on life, we have the power through Jesus Christ not to give in to these invitations to disobey God.

The devil

The previous chapter dealt with Satan, the god of this world, so I won't take time to repeat what I have already said. But just remember, the devil will use any type of attractive or not-so-attractive ideas, concepts, methods, or attitudes to influence our thinking and get us to live independent of God. As strong as the devil's pull may be, though, God is all-powerful, and if we rely on Him, we will have the ability to withstand the attacks the enemy launches at our minds.

POWER VS. TRUTH

Satan is not only a clever enemy, but an intelligent one as well. He knows and understands that the key to victory in the spiritual battle for our minds is truth rather than power. Let me explain.

I've met some well-meaning Christians who somehow have the wrong idea that God has recruited them to be "devil busters"—to go around kicking Satan in the bum! As exciting as it may sound to be a "Terminator for Truth," it's not biblical. Nowhere in God's Word will you find that some kind of spiritual power confrontation with the forces of darkness will set you free. God does not want us running around picking fights with the devil and his demons—you'll lose! The Lord wants us to fight the battle His way, and with His help.

God instructs us to stand firm, resist the devil, and he will flee from us (Ephesians 6:13–14; James 4:7). Victory and freedom will come when we confront the powers of darkness with the truth. What is truth? Basically, truth means that the facts conform to reality; truth identifies things as they are. For example: $3 \times 3 = 9$; $2 + 2 = 4$; a red traffic light always means stop. Most people would agree that these concepts are true. However, we live in a relative-truth culture that encourages us to look at spiritual and moral truth differently. In a national survey, 70 percent of the teens surveyed said they believe there is no such thing as "absolute truth."[3] In other words, two people could define truth in conflicting ways and both could still be correct. When you think about this attitude toward truth, it doesn't make logical sense. Just think about the simple math illustrations above.

Truth by its very definition is narrow. Philosophers say truth is an idea. Webster's says truth is "The state of being the case; the body of real things, events and facts." The Bible says that ultimately truth is found in Jesus, who said, "I am the way, the truth, and the life" (John 14:6).

The facts are that Satan is a liar; he distorts and twists truth every chance he gets. There is no truth in him (John 8:44). He is a deceiver and works cleverly to mislead us. He knows that if he can get us to believe a lie, then he can get us to live that lie. Here's a sample of some of the more common lies he uses with teens today:

+ Money and bling will make you happy. "Get all the stuff you can!"
+ Sex is okay, as long as it's safe and consensual.
+ Looks are everything.
+ It's okay to drink and get drunk, just don't drive.
+ Follow the crowd and you're never alone.
+ You're not here for a long time, just a good time.
+ You're a product of evolution.
+ There's no such thing as absolute truth.
+ All religions lead to God.
+ You're a loser. You'll never be successful.
+ There are no long-term consequences for the choices you make.
+ God has a lousy plan for your life.

Satan's power is in his abundance of lies, but he is defeated and his plans fall apart when we confront him with the truth of God through His Word. God is trustworthy and cannot lie (Titus 1:2; Hebrews 6:18).

God promises to keep us from the Evil One by teaching us His words of truth (John 17:15, 17). Therefore, our power as believers is in knowing the truth. Jesus said that when you know the truth, the truth will set you free (John 8:32). When we know the divine truth from God, we will be free from the power of sin and the constant search for meaning and purpose.

But how can we know and understand truth? Once we put our faith and trust in Christ, God sends His Spirit to live within us and to guide us into all truth (John 16:13). And then it's up to us to take time to get to know God's personality, studying the Bible, and being doers of the Word (James 1:22). Many Christians today are living defeated lives because they don't know what the Bible actually teaches, so they can't expose the devil's lies with the truth.

It's also our responsibility as believers to focus our minds on what is true (Philippians 4:8). In a world like ours, that's tough to do. Using God's Word as a filter for what we feed our minds—comparing everything we see, read, or hear to what the Bible teaches—enables us to choose the truth over a lie. Everyone needs a biblical worldview.

Don't be deceived into thinking that just because you're a Christian, Satan is no longer interested in manipulating your life through your mind. It's *because* you're a Christian that he'll try even harder. He knows that if he can direct your thoughts, he can ultimately direct your behavior, tempting you to live without God. Take a look at how he influenced the following people.

In 1 Chronicles 21:1, we read that Satan rose up against Israel and incited David to take a census of Israel. John 13:2 says that the devil prompted Judas to betray Jesus. And in Acts 5:3 Peter confronts Ananias: "Why have you let Satan fill your heart? You lied to the Holy Spirit, and you kept some of the money for yourself."

Be careful to guard your thoughts, and don't allow Satan to influence your behavior.

Satan's Battle for the Minds of Teens

As we've said, Satan's battle for the minds of teens begins in movies, the Internet, books, peer pressure, video and computer games, music, and other sources. The battle also wages in baiting teens to become involved in occult-related activities.

In a national study of teens done by the Barna Research Group, it was discovered that 79 percent had read or looked at their horoscope.[4] Over 30 percent of teens had read a book about witchcraft or Wicca, used a Ouija board, or had their palms read. A smaller percentage had played a game that featured witchcraft or psychic elements, had their fortune told, had been physically present when someone was using his psychic or supernatural powers, or had participated in a séance.

Perhaps you think that Christian teens would have different answers. However, as part of the research for this book, we did an informal survey of more than nine hundred students in different Christian schools and churches. Keep in mind these are all solid groups that teach the Bible and center their ministry on Jesus. Yet we found a surprising number of teens who struggle with bad thoughts about God; have experienced a presence that scared them; found it mentally hard to pray and read the Bible; have heard "voices" in their head, like there was a subconscious-self talking to them; or have frequently had thoughts of suicide or impulsive violent thoughts.

Do you struggle with some of the same things these surveyed teens struggle with? You don't need to be frightened. You can change what's happening on the battlefield of your mind! It starts by choosing the truth over the Enemy's lies moment by moment. Memorizing Scripture is a great way to remember to choose truth. Each verse can be thrown at a frightening or distressful thought when it pops into your mind.

Be aware that Satan uses more than occult practices or scary/distracting thoughts to gain a foothold to confuse, oppress, and seduce us; there are also things that aren't really evil that give him access to our minds.

HOW THE DEVIL GETS A FOOTHOLD
IN YOUR LIFE

The first time I went rock climbing I thought I was going to die! My first mistake was to go with some guys who are like spiders in their ability to climb the faces of huge rocks. My second mistake was not recognizing my own limitations. My strength gave out halfway up this humongous rock, and it became increasingly difficult to keep going. I tried to figure out if there'd be more pain if I kept climbing or if I let go and fell to the hard ground below! The hardest part of the climb for me was finding cracks, crevasses, and little ledges where I could get a foothold or some kind of grip with a finger or two. Without them, I wouldn't have been able to move farther up.

The devil is looking for some little ledge, crack, or crevasse he can use to gain access to our thinking. Some of these footholds are pretty obvious and in-your-face, while others are more sly.

Before we start looking at these, I want to be clear about something. This part of the chapter isn't supposed to be some sort of list that tells you what you should and should not be doing, watching, reading, or involving yourself in. And just because you don't find something on this list doesn't mean that it's okay to be involved in it. Rather, I want you to use the information to carefully examine your participation in anything you do. Stop and objectively consider what you're putting into your mind and how it could be affecting your thinking and the way you live your life. Use the Bible, prayer, and godly counsel as your filter. Now let me challenge your thinking!

Party games

Bloody Mary has been a popular party game for many years. A common version of the game requires someone to go into a completely darkened bathroom alone, spin around six times, face the mirror, and call upon Bloody Mary to show herself—which she may do. Other versions are just as inviting to demonic powers. This game may seem innocent or like a cute trick. But in reality it is giving yourself casual exposure to the occult. It can be a very dangerous first step into the world of darkness.

Ouija boards (the name is a combination of the French and German words for *yes*) have been around in various forms for hundreds of years. The modern version by Parker Brothers is a game board with the numbers zero through nine, the alphabet, and the words *good, bye, yes,* and *no* printed on the surface. A teardrop-shaped pointer is placed on the board.

Two players face each other over the board with their fingers lightly resting on the pointer, allowing it to move freely. The players ask questions relating to things like career, marriage, and health and wait for the pointer to spell out answers. The game has also been used for contacting the dead and the spirit realm, developing psychic powers, and finding lost things. It's a mystery how or why the game works, even to the manufacturer. I'm sure some of it is due to muscle twitching, but you can't deny that demonic powers are also involved.

Most who play with this seemingly innocent game have no idea what they are dealing with. The Ouija board is clearly a form of divination (fortune-telling and guidance), which is forbidden by the Bible (Deuteronomy 18:10; Isaiah 65:11; Acts 16:16–18).

Automatic writing is practiced by people who call themselves spiritual mediums. These people enter a trance and write down any words or impressions that come to mind. This practice is an obvious counterfeit of the prophetic voice of God. The difference is that God works through the active minds of His people, but occult practices require a passive state of mind. The occult actually bypasses the mind and the personality of the person involved, and a different personality emerges. God *never* does this, but instead always uses the inherent personality and gifts of each person He created.

Tarot cards are often regarded as the ancestor of modern playing cards. They are commonly used for divination by having a person choose cards from the deck, then having them read by the "expert."

Palm reading or palmistry is the study and interpretation of the distinguishing features of the palm of the hand. Palm readers look at line patterns on the palm and the color and texture of the skin. People feel that by having their palms read they will gain insight into the future. The Bible reminds us in the Old Testament book of Isaiah that we should consult God regarding such matters (8:19–20).

Spirit guides are nothing more than demonic voices. People invite these to invade their body and personality in a variety of ways.

Blood pacts are common in satanic ceremonies, where they draw blood and drink it. This is an obvious counterfeit to the work Jesus did on the cross by shedding His blood. Only the blood of Jesus shed for our salvation brings power to our lives.

We've hardly begun to expose the social activities with satanic and occult connections. And keep in mind that things change every year—what's available, what's popular, and what's not. Thus, you need to guard yourself against a diversion that appears to be harmless entertainment but that, in reality, may be the first step into the Enemy's camp. Seriously look at the advice God gives us in Deuteronomy 18:10–13:

> Never sacrifice your son or daughter as a burnt offering. And do
> not let your people practice fortune-telling, or use sorcery, or

interpret omens, or engage in witchcraft, or cast spells, or function as mediums or psychics, or call forth the spirits of the dead. Anyone who does these things is detestable to the Lord. It is because the other nations have done these detestable things that the Lord your God will drive them out ahead of you. But you must be blameless before the Lord your God.

Web sites

Cyberspace is filled with everything imaginable when it comes to Satan and the occult. The Internet is probably one of the most spiritually dangerous places for teens. Hazardous information is readily available and becomes easily addictive. You can spend literally hours exploring one site after another and, without realizing it, find yourself slipping deeper and deeper into darkness.

Remember the Internet is a tool—it can be used for evil or good. Fifty-two percent of teens use the Internet every day.[5] But there are also a ton of positive sites to be found in cyberspace, including lots that can help you grow spiritually. One thing you may want to think about is installing some filtering software on your computer. That way you won't get somewhere you don't want to be by accident, and on a day when you might feel weak, you will be protected by the software. Don't ever forget how important it is to protect your mind!

Computer games

Video and computer game manufacturers are making billions of dollars. While not all games are evil, some can subtly lure us into the kingdom of darkness. Here are just a few examples of games that dabble in occult themes. If these are in your collection, you may want to ditch them.

Devil May Cry 4
Guild Wars: Nightfall
Overlord
Monster Madness: Battle for Suburbia
Neverwinter Nights 2
F.E.A.R.

Once again, these games just scratch the surface of the ones already on the market, let alone those that will be available in the future. Be on your guard with the themes of mysticism, vampires, and demons, as well as blood, guts, and violence. Games like these are more than just entertainment. Through them, Satan can be given an opportunity to influence your thoughts.

And be careful of role-playing games like Dungeons & Dragons. In this game, players use sorcery and witchcraft to achieve their objectives. A practicing witch considered the game such a good tool for instructing people in paganism that he wrote a special manual showing players how to move from the game to real sorcery.

Books and magazines

Books have been gateways into the occult for millions of readers. Seventeen-year-old Eric told me that he liked books better than DVDs or movies to feed his hunger for violence and the occult. He could create more graphic pictures in his mind from what he read than he could find on the screen.

There are countless books about things like witchcraft, sorcery, vampires, and divination. They can be blatant or have occult subjects quietly woven into the background. And don't be fooled by fiction books on the same subjects. Fiction stories about the same topics can allow the Enemy access to your mind faster and more subtly than nonfiction books.

We've already discussed being aware of magazines like *Revolver* and *Thrasher*, but let's not leave out comics. Superheroes have gotten darker and sometimes sinister. Even actor Nicolas Cage and his son, Weston, are adding to the catalog of darkness with their new comic book, *Voodoo Child*—the first of six issues.

Reading is a great thing to expand your mind. Just use some discretion, based on biblical truth, when choosing a book or other literature.

Movies and DVDs

If you're like me, you enjoy going to the movies or renting DVDs. Again, we just need to show some discretion about what we watch. Whether it's a slasher flick or something a little less gory, many films have the potential to desensitize us to evil, violence, immoral sex, witchcraft, and the occult. A steady diet of the following kinds of movies with occult elements can make you a much easier target for Satan's schemes. Past movies have been:

+ *Ghostrider*
+ *Skinwalkers*
+ *Harry Potter and the Order of the Phoenix*
+ *Darkness Falls*
+ *Final Fantasy*
+ *The Mothman Prophecies*
+ *The Others*
+ *Dreamcatcher*
+ *The Ring*
+ *Sleepy Hollow*
+ *The Haunting*
+ *What Lies Beneath*
+ *Stardust*

There have been even comedies with occult elements. Remember: Be cautious about being disarmed to spiritual dangers with laughter.

Consider as well the Saturday morning cartoon characters Casper the Friendly Ghost and the Great Dane Scooby-Doo, who made a brief move to the big screen. In the movie, Scooby-Doo and the kids of Mystery, Inc., are reunited at a spooky amusement park/college hot spot on an island to figure out why college students are turning into zombies. The movie is filled with occult elements.

I'm not saying all movies are bad. There have been some good things produced and some positive new films released. We just need to be selective in what we watch by using a biblical filter.

TV

Television has become a significant value-shaper in our country. Teens spend an average of four to six hours per day interacting with the mass media in various forms. Eighty-nine percent watch television each day.[6] Studies indicate that the average student will have watched seventeen thousand hours of television and seen eighteen thousand simulated murders before graduating from high school.

In the last few years, there's been a dramatic increase in the number of weekly prime-time shows, cable programs, and made-for-TV movies with occult elements and the occasional trip into the world of darkness. There have been shows like *Ghost Whisper, Medium, Angel, Moonlight, Crossing Over with John Edward,* and WB's *Supernatural.* Sorcery, spells, power beams, incantations, ESP, crystal powers, and telepathy can be found everywhere, even in Saturday morning cartoons.

And let's remember that this darkness can also come in the form of empty philosophies, violence, and immorality. Talk shows, soap operas, and music videos ooze with it. Shows like MTV's *Jackass* and *The Osbournes* and HBO's *Sex and the City* and *The Sopranos* more than crossed the line. Sex and homosexuality have been popularized with former shows like *NYPD Blue*, *Will and Grace*, and *Queer Eye for the Straight Guy*. More are sure to arise with each coming season.

Next time you turn on the TV, take a moment to think about what you'll be watching. And don't be afraid to use the remote control to find something that's spiritually healthy for you to watch.

Music

Research confirms that music may be the single most identifiable cultural creation of a generation. It's a special form of communication that's theirs forever. Music is important in teens' lives, having incredible influence and devouring large amounts of time and money—as well as the mind.

The roots of occult themes in contemporary music can be traced to some of rock's earliest stars. The Rolling Stones recorded songs like "Sympathy for the Devil," "Their Satanic Majesty's Request," and "Goat's Head Soup" (a severed goat's head is used in satanic worship). Former Black Sabbath lead singer Ozzy Osbourne sang openly of demons in "Devil's Daughter." Ozzy would later enjoy the spotlight on TV as a very abnormal husband and father.

The lyrics of current heavy metal and black metal bands are even more perverse and satanic, dealing with such topics as the death of God, sitting at Satan's left hand, calling Jesus the deceiver, human sacrifice, and glorifying the names of Satan. And the lyrics are getting through. An Arkansas teen attempted to kill his parents under the inspiration of a song by a thrash metal band. He said he consulted a Ouija board and heard voices telling him to murder his parents. Police found occult-themed music queued up in his stereo.

In the next chapter we will take more time to discuss the importance of being discerning in the music we listen to, because the lyrics do matter.

Drugs and alcohol

Drug and alcohol abuse has reached epidemic proportions in our society, especially among students. Ecstasy and the rave scene are huge problems. Why? Partly because substance abuse temporarily dulls the pain and the pressures of life. Substance abuse gives a false sense of security and seems more reliable than people.

It's no coincidence that the rise in occult activity among students parallels the rise in substance abuse. There is a definite link between the two (although not everyone using drugs is involved in the occult). But drugs can be an entryway to the occult. Even when substance abuse is not directly linked to the occult, it destroys your relationship with the one true God who *is* reliable, *is* secure, and walks through the pain and pressures of life *with* you (Isaiah 43:1–3).

Satan's goal is to capture your mind, and substances that alter your mind leave you vulnerable to his influence and control. A fifteen-year-old girl summed it up this way: "Taking drugs is like getting into a strange car with a strange person and going down a road you've never been before."

School

Another opportunity for the devil to gain a foothold in your mind is in the classroom. "Values clarification" is a big part of education today. It's actually just another way of saying there's no such thing as absolute truth. That means there are no such things as unmovable moral values regarding sex before marriage, alternative lifestyles, and honesty. It means you can believe and do whatever you want because it's your truth—no matter how it may affect someone else.

If absolute truth does not exist, then we don't have to obey traffic laws anymore if we decide it's not our truth. Instead of purchasing things in the store, you can steal them if paying for something isn't part of your truth. This sounds ridiculous, but that's essentially what's being subtly taught in some classrooms. (We'll talk more about New Age beliefs in chapter 8.) Remember, if Satan can get you to believe a lie, even in the classroom, then he can get you to live it.

Clothing

For many people, clothing, hairstyle, and makeup are an outward sign of an inward struggle for significance, acceptance, and security—their identity. And some of today's fashions seem to encourage a step into the darkness to meet those needs.

In a Southern California mall not far from my office is a trendy store geared for teens. More than 95 percent of the items in the store are adorned with satanic and occult symbols (see appendix A for a list of these symbols). They are on belts, scarves, jewelry, T-shirts, ties, pants, hats, and even socks. Beware of two dangers involved in wearing clothes and other fashion articles with satanic and occult symbols. First, the symbols represent values and a lifestyle that are contrary to the things of God. Second, as you search for ways to deal with the issues you face in day-to-day living, the devil can entice you to experiment with these symbols to see if they really have any power. Sometimes you may get more than you bargained for!

Don't take your fashion cues from an Abercrombie & Fitch catalog or from a female pop singer who chooses to flaunt more skin than clothing. Showing skin may gain a lot of attention—but not the attention you really want or need. And you might very well attract attention in a way that also entices you to participate in things you know would damage your relationship with God.

There's nothing wrong with wanting to be hip and in style—just do it in a way that is pleasing to God.

Anger and unforgiveness

Maybe you don't really struggle with the temptation to play around with mind-altering chemicals or occult practices. And maybe you have a pretty good handle on what God would be pleased with in the area of entertainment and fashion. But the devil still has some other ways to gain a foothold in your life and infiltrate your thinking.

One of those is through anger. There are times when it is okay to be angry, as long as that anger does not turn into sin (Ephesians 4:26). We should be angry about the evil, injustice, and immorality in the world. The Bible says that even Jesus got angry (see Matthew 21:12 and John 2:15). But anger that is selfish, vindictive, bitter, resentful, and uncontrolled can give Satan the opportunity to work his way into our minds to manipulate and control us, ultimately allowing us to be consumed by our feelings of anger.

There's another method the Enemy uses that's closely tied to anger: unforgiveness. This is Satan's greatest avenue of access to all Christians—young and mature. Even if you have no other link to the occult in your life, an attitude of unforgiveness can turn into bitterness, becoming like a cancer to your spirit, making you an easy target for Satan's influence. Paul urges us to forgive one another "so that Satan will not outsmart us. For we are familiar with his evil schemes" (2 Corinthians 2:11).

THE DAПGER OF DABBLIПG

A tragic story, one that shows how dabbling can be dangerous, may be the best way to finish this chapter. We must never underestimate the cunning skill of the Enemy and how subtly he can lead us down the wrong path. Sometimes it starts with a game, a book, or a drug. And once Satan is given an opportunity, there's no telling how things will end up.

Jim Hardy, a high school student from Missouri, came from a rotten home situation. He wanted security, acceptance, and especially power to change his life. He started dabbling a little bit in the occult with things like Ouija boards and some role-playing games. He also experimented with drugs. In the process he found himself connecting with a new source of power—the devil.

Two of his friends joined him, and the drug abuse moved from marijuana to cocaine to heroin. Together they experimented with the power of darkness by becoming frequently involved in occult practices. As they fed their minds on a variety of extremely violent and occult movies and books, they started hearing voices. People at school were afraid of them because of their power and the things they were rumored to be involved in.

Finally the voices in their heads said, "It is time. Kill someone." Then the voices told them that their classmate Steven

Newberry was the "one." The plan was to lure the mentally slow boy into their group with drugs. Because Steven wanted to be accepted like everybody else, he started getting high with Jim and the others.

One night they invited Steven to join them in some occult practices in the woods. After getting high, Jim and his two friends told Steven to lead them down a trail. Within a few minutes Jim and his friends heard the voices again. This time they said, "Now. Do it now." So they did. Then they threw his lifeless body down an abandoned well.

After they were caught, the police asked the boys why they did such a horrible thing. Their cold-blooded response was, "We did it for our lord and master, Satan."

This story is shocking—and sad. And what's alarming is that Jim's involvement in the occult started out as innocent dabbling, like so many students are doing today. You may be thinking that there's no way you would ever murder someone. But I don't think Jim or his two friends thought their experimenting with the occult would lead them to take someone else's life either.

If you or someone you know is struggling with questions about a certain activity, first go to God through prayer and your Bible. Also enlist your parents, a youth group leader, or a trusted friend for advice. Don't try to wrestle through it alone. Get help before things get out of control.

We've covered a lot of ground in this chapter—everything from truth confrontations to footholds that Satan will try to gain. I hope what we've discussed has caused you to think about what you are putting into your mind and about the possible consequences. Remember, not everything targeted at you is good for you.

Learn to be more discerning and selective about what goes in, based on the truth of God's Word. As Paul wrote in Ephesians

4:27 NIV, "Do not give the devil a foothold," especially in your mind. Always remember that Satan is a powerful foe. We may be able to humanly control some of our thoughts, but there's no way we can defeat the Enemy on our own. The battle to influence and control our thinking is real, but we can experience victory in this battle when we choose God's Word and His truth rather than Satan's lie.

Think about it

1. What lies has Satan been trying to infiltrate your mind with? What does the Bible specifically say about these things?

   After checking with God's Word about each lie, make a two-column list on a piece of paper, one side with the lie and the other with God's truth. Take time to read and think about each one. Then commit all of this to the Lord in prayer. Specifically ask God to help you live those truths.

2. Take a few minutes to make a list of your favorite songs, DVDs, TV shows, and Web sites. Now compare each one of their themes with what the Bible teaches in Philippians 4:8. How do they measure up?

   If you find that God would not be pleased with some of the things you have been filling your mind with, think about what else you could do with your time to feed your mind on more positive things.

3. Are you angry or bitter toward someone else? What happened that caused these feelings? Spend some time in prayer, asking God to help you have a better attitude about each situation and by forgiving that person. Pray that He will enable you to go to that person and tell them

you forgive them. Ask God to help you move ahead in your life.

As you work through the things we've discussed in this chapter, don't hesitate to ask a trusted friend to pray along with you and to keep you accountable for the changes that you need to make.

So far in this book we've been talking about who Satan is, what he does, and the kind of battle that we're in. And it's important to understand that stuff so you'll know what you're up against. In the next part we'll be talking about several specific ways Satan can influence you—sometimes without your knowing it. He has a plan to sidetrack us through subtle (and sometimes not so subtle) means. Once we understand these strategies of Satan, we can learn to take control.

PART TWO
WAYS SATAN CAN
GET TO YOU

CHAPTER 5

HOW IS MUSIC
CHANGING YOUR LIFE?

Have you ever dreamed of being a rock star? Now you can experience the rush of being a rock hero—that is, if you're into guitar. And the cost is relatively cheap. You don't have to move to a big city to make it in the "biz," and you don't have to lay out a lot of cash for gear and lessons. In fact, you don't even have to spend hours in your room practicing. All you need to do is get a PlayStation 2, a game controller that resembles a tiny Gibson SG, and Guitar Hero 2 software. You'll be shredding heavy metal guitar licks in less than fifteen minutes.

Guitar Hero has become a cultural phenomenon after more than two million "ax slingers" have bought the software. All you have to do to unlock some monster guitar licks is to press the right-colored button at the right time. You can then experience the illusion that you are actually playing these licks yourself. But Guitar Hero 2 isn't just for amateurs. *The New York Times* reported that Ed Robertson, lead guitarist for the Barenaked Ladies, was so engrossed in a Guitar Hero solo of "Free Bird" that he barely made it onstage for a real concert.[1]

My dream to become a big-time rocker took a bit more effort to achieve. I saw it as a way to get everything I wanted in life: fame, money, fast cars, and women. In seventh grade I bought my first drum set with money I had saved up from a paper route. I started playing in a band that same year for parties, school dances, and grand openings of stores. By the time I was a junior in high school I was playing professionally, opening in concert for bands like Fleetwood Mac and Santana. Eventually I ended up playing in some of the top nightclubs on the West Coast, doing some studio work, and giving private drum lessons. The drums are still a big part of my life and ministry—especially when I speak on public middle school and high school campuses. I'm even endorsed by major equipment companies like DW Drums, Vic Firth sticks, Evans heads, and SABIAN cymbals.

As you might have guessed, I am a music fanatic. While doing gigs at concerts and recording sessions, playing Broadway touring shows, and working in nightclubs, I had the opportunity to play a lot of different styles of music. Over the years I've acquired a huge collection of music that I like listening to.

So relax. I'm not out to attack your favorite groups or motivate you to attend a CD-smashing party. But I do want you to carefully think about the music you listen to and the effect it could be having on your attitudes and actions.

In this chapter we will take a look at some of the issues and concerns related to music. We'll also see how Satan is using false teaching through and about music to misguide us, and how to establish standards for what we should and should not listen to.

THE POWER OF MUSIC

Music is one of the most powerful and underestimated influences in the lives of teens. It's like a private language for every generation. Music has the power to alter our opinions, attitudes, values, beliefs, relationships, and lifestyle choices.[2] But a lot of teens don't recognize how powerful this influence is in their lives. It becomes a dangerous blind spot. Everywhere we go and in just about everything we do, we are surrounded by music. Teens spend an average of four to six hours per day interacting with mass media of different forms. When it comes to music, 94 percent listen to the radio, and 91 percent play CDs or iPods every day.[3]

We live in a music-saturated culture. Not only do we listen to it on mp3 players, on computers, and in our cars, but also it's in the stores where we shop, in the restaurants where we eat, and in the movies we watch. Can you imagine how dull an adventure film would be without the musical background to add excitement? Where would the heroes be without their theme songs? What about an extreme sports show without music?

Studies have revealed that the average student listens to more than ten thousand hours of music between the seventh and twelfth grades, and that doesn't include watching thousands of hours of MTV or VH1! Anything we are exposed to this much has got to have an influence on us.

Eighteen-year-old Todd says that music is the most important thing in his life: "The CDs, concerts, lights, the whole atmosphere—it's my salvation. If things bother me, I'll go into my room and lock the door, turn on the stereo, and escape into my own world. I can just space. Music is a lot cheaper than drugs, and it's legal. I'm a music freak! It's the place I'm the happiest. So why not indulge my music habit, even though it takes most of my cash? It's better than a drug habit or some other form of meaningless entertainment."

We identify with music, and it helps us to express our feelings, problems, joys, and beliefs. Music reflects and directs our culture. It often tells the story of our times, highlighting the struggles and issues facing our society, such as abortion, racial tension, violence, and AIDS.

Some musicians or groups attempt to do outrageous stunts onstage to make a point. Some will claim they aren't doing it for attention—they are only standing up for what they believe in.

Take, for example, a concert that was scheduled to take place in St. Petersburg, Florida, by a hard-rock band called Hell on Earth. The group had planned to feature an onstage suicide of a terminally ill person during their concert to raise awareness of so-called right-to-die issues. The band is known for outrageous stunts like chocolate syrup wrestling and grinding up live rats in a blender.

Bandleader Billy Tourtelot sent an email out to fans the week before the concert and said, "This show is far more than a typical Hell on Earth performance. This is about standing up for what you believe in, and I am a strong supporter of physician-assisted suicide." In response to the band's plan, the city council approved an emergency ordinace, making it illegal to conduct a suicide for commercial or entertainment purposes and to host, promote, and sell tickets for such an event. The owner of the Palace Theater in downtown St. Petersburg then canceled the concert.

I'm all for speaking out on issues in our culture, but I also think there's an appropriate way to address each problem. In this situation, Hell on Earth should have found a better way to express their feelings.

For millions of teens, music produces lifestyles to adopt and cultural heroes to look up to and imitate. Singers, songwriters, and bands often set the pace for a variety of trends that influence the way we dress, what we think, and what we do. Preteen girls are clamoring to dress and act like today's pop stars and celebutantes. Guys all over the country started wearing their hats backward, their pants baggy, and their posture a strong, "cool" slouch based on the hip-hop scene and the rappers they see. Even their fingers and hand signs imitate the most popular musicians. Slang changes with popular songs. *Bling* is a word not recognized by a lot of adults, but it is recognized by a majority of teens.

In the lyrics, musicians are teachers trying to communicate a message about how we should live. And a lot of teens I meet have been listening to these messages. Just look at how the whole Goth or hip-hop scenes started and what they have become.

Goth used to be a subclassification of punk music, but it gradually emerged as a subculture of its own, complete with its own music, graphic art, literature, and fashion. Because there's so much diversity within the gothic world, its members strongly resist any attempts at defining labels. The same thing happened with hip-hop.

In ancient history, the term *gothic* started out as a synonym for "uncivilized and barbaric." Then in the Middle Ages people assumed gothic meant "dark and ominous." The mysterious and macabre literature of the late nineteenth century, like Mary Shelley's *Frankenstein* and Bram Stoker's *Dracula*, was called gothic because of the ominous imagery. Then it expanded to include the ghoulish. Jump ahead in history to the 1970s and early 1980s, when punk bands were taking a more stark, somber, and ghostly direction, and the British press extended the term to music because of the association with the literature. Today the term is applied to the people who listen to the music.

Basically, Goth celebrates the dark recesses of the human psyche. It focuses on dark sensuality, sweeping sadness, and morbid fascination with forbidden love and the beauty of enduring pain. There are a lot of teens who lead unhappy, unachieved lives, which is sad. Goth makes depression and angst a lifestyle choice—which some would say makes it art. Goth has been described as a self-deflating culture that delights in self-parody and in ridiculing itself. Those involved say it's fun. The music defines what those involved believe and how they live.

The real issue

At the time I wrote this book, the top three most popular genres of music listed by teens surveyed were rap/hip-hop, rock, and R&B. The least favorite style of all was country.[4] But things can change almost overnight. When you really think about the way music can influence us, it's not the style that we need to worry about.

The real issue we need to deal with is the lyrics. We need to carefully examine the philosophies songs are promoting. Colossians 2:8 says, "Don't let anyone capture you with empty philosophies and high-sounding nonsense that come from human thinking and from the spiritual powers of this world, rather than from Christ." You can find these deceptive philosophies and negative messages no matter what style of music you listen to, including country, rap/hip-hop, urban, punk, R&B, funk, reggae, thrash metal, rave, top 40, alternative, rhythmic, Latin, and classic rock. Even the most mellow of adult easy listening can have immoral or empty lyrics. Anyone who pays attention to the lyrics can hear the prominent themes of sex, violence, rebellion, suicide, and the occult. Sometimes the truth is twisted so subtly that unless you pay close attention, you can easily be deceived.

Some secular music also bears a core message of hopelessness. It discusses problems in the world but never offers any solutions. If we listen to these messages long enough, we will start to believe there is no hope. And when you lose your hope, you'll do just about anything.

To see the effect these messages are having, all you have to do is pick up a magazine, watch the news, or look around your school. While music can't *make* you do something, its philosophies can shape your thoughts, attitudes, and philosophy of life. And those beliefs eventually affect your behavior. A nineteen-year-old girl in Florida, who shot and killed a German tourist, said her inspiration to murder came from a rap song. Music is not the only thing causing these problems, but it's definitely one of the big contributing factors involving teens.

"Inspirational" rap music has become extremely popular; artists like Kanye West, 50 Cent, Sean Paul, Ludacris, Eve, and Shop Boyz are just a handful of names that get tremendous airplay. And we can't look at this genre without mentioning Eminem. His lyrics are full of dazzling escapades that delve into the mind of a violently warped and vulgar songwriter. Some say he has written some of the most demented lyrics ever recorded. "I do say things that I think will shock people," he says. "But I don't do things to shock people. I'm not trying to be the next Tupac, but I don't know how long I'm going to be on this planet. So while I'm here, I might as well make the most of it."[5]

But Eminem is not the only artist who tries to outrage people. How about shock-rocker Marilyn Manson? No music discussion would be complete without mentioning the former Brian Warner, known for his ghastly cadaverous look with makeup and body piercings. Manson's music encourages drug abuse, violence, hatred, death, and suicide. In some cities, his concerts have drawn protests because of his controversial macabre lyrics and outrageous stage behavior. Some people even believe his music influenced the teenage gunmen in the Columbine High School massacre.

The members of Slipknot, originally from Des Moines, Iowa, are angry and loud. They wear industrial-style jumpsuits and gruesome masks, and the members identify themselves by numbers instead of names. Slipknot devotees have dubbed themselves "maggots" and see Slipknot's music as a means to escape the pain of life. The band's vocalist, Corey Taylor (#8), says their album *Iowa* is dark and dangerous. For the title track, "Iowa,"

Taylor even stripped down naked and cut himself up before recording it.[6]

Even though Marilyn Manson was raised in the Episcopal Church and went to a nondenominational Christian school, he says he identifies with Satan. "I started to seek out other interpretations of God. And initially, when you rebel, you go for the obvious choices—heavy metal, Satanism. To me, Satan ultimately represents rebellion. Lucifer was the angel that was kicked out of heaven because he wanted to be God. To me, what greater character to identify with?"[7]

In no way am I saying that Eminem, Marilyn Manson, or Slipknot are Satan worshipers, but do you see how subtly the devil is using their music—and that of many other artists—to promote his lies? Satan will do everything he can to pervert and dilute God's truth, especially in such a powerful medium as music.

Not all secular music is bad or satanic. A secular performer who doesn't know the Lord can perform music that doesn't contradict what the Bible teaches. A performer may sing about life in a positive way that gets us to think and perhaps make positive changes in our lives. And not all Christian music is good. Sometimes artists are singing about God on a Christian record label but their lyrics are not accurate to what the Bible teaches. Or their personal lives are a disaster.

So how are you supposed to sort all this out? First, learn to evaluate music on the timeless principles found in God's Word. In 1 Thessalonians 5:21, the apostle Paul encourages us to test everything (which obviously includes the music we listen to) against the truth and standard of the Bible. Just because an artist or a group is not displaying occult symbols on their albums or identifying with the devil does not mean the content of their songs is something God would want us to feed our minds on.

And likewise, don't be too quick to call someone a Christian just because he or she is dedicating an album to God or using some Christian buzzword. Don't be misled by some rock star wearing a cross, dedicating an album to God, praying before a concert, or thanking Him for an award. I distinctly remember signing autographs before I was a Christian with "God Bless You," only because it looked good. I had no clue at that time what it meant or who God really was.

Second, try to discern whether someone's lifestyle really matches what he or she is singing. We also need to find out if they are talking about the "god of this world" or the God of the Bible. Check to see if their talk matches their walk. In the book of Ephesians, the apostle Paul talks about the lifestyle of one who is a true follower of Jesus. He writes, "I, a prisoner for serving the Lord, beg you to lead a life worthy of your calling, for you have been called by God" (4:1). Then in the next chapter he says, "For once you were full of darkness, but now you have light from the Lord. So live as people of light!" (5:8). In other words, to claim that you are a Christian—someone who follows Jesus—there must have been a change that took place in your life. You can't talk about God for seventy-five minutes at church on Sunday morning and then mock Him the rest of the week.

Only God truly knows the hearts of any band members, but it's pretty obvious by their lyrics and lifestyles that many are singing and living messages that are contrary to what the Bible teaches. In Matthew 12:34 we read, "Whatever is in your heart determines what you say."

As we discovered in a previous chapter, Satan loves to confuse and frustrate. He enjoys mixed messages, such as an ungodly musician wearing a cross and half-truths, such as a so-called Christian group singing unbiblical lyrics. We've already established that he wields a lot of power in the area of music, so let's take a quick look at what Satan can and cannot do in regard to the music you're listening to.

HOW SATAN CAN USE MUSIC

There's a legend that says the iconic blues guitarist Robert Johnson was granted his unbelievable "otherworldly" chops by the devil himself in a deal struck at a crossroads in Mississippi. The cost was his soul. But that's as legend has it. Stuff like that doesn't really happen. No one would actually do some crazy thing for Satan because of music . . . *would they?*

Slayer was just another Los Angeles–area garage band that wanted to make it big. They went to a management company, which advised them to act as if they worshiped Satan—it would help them go straight to the top. That's just what they did, and they have been a strong influence on the death/thrash metal scene for years.

Fans Jacob Delashmutt, Joseph Fiorella, and Royce Casey were into drugs and spent a lot of time hanging out and studying the lyrics to the former garage band's songs. As they listened, they decided to follow what the music told them to do.

On a warm July day Jacob, Joseph, and Royce killed fifteen-year-old Elyse Pahler. They acted out the song lyrics in hopes it would make their own death-metal band successful.

There are a number of groups that are into Satan, use occult symbols, and write songs that glorify the devil. Because of society's hero worship of musicians, these people are leading their followers down a path to hell. And even those who just pretend they are into Satan so they can sell their music and concert DVDs or just lead ungodly lives are used like pawns in the hands of the Enemy to deceive, confuse, frustrate, and mislead. Proverbs 17:4 says, "Wrongdoers eagerly listen to gossip; liars pay close attention to slander." The only way to know what is right and not become a victim of someone's misguided philosophies of life is to study and know God's Word.

Along with Satan's influence comes a lot of confusion about his role in music.

Music TV

Unless you were born in a cave in Siberia, you know that MTV is Music Television. It's the music authority, where teens and young adults turn to find out what's happening and what's next in music and pop culture. MTV reaches 412 million households worldwide and is the number one media brand in the world. It gives viewers music that defines a generation. MTV also gives young adults advice on everything they are passionate about, including attitude, fashion, lifestyle, sports, politics, and creativity, all through the prism of music.

Check out the power of MTV and see if you agree with what they say about their influence on your generation:

1. Young adults ages twelve to thirty-four name MTV as the most recognized network. In fact, MTV is the best way to connect with these people, who are ninety-five million strong and growing, representing 32 percent of the population. They look to MTV to find out about their world in their language, from their point of view.
2. The MTV audience wields more than $250 billion in buying power. By the year 2010, young-adult spending power is projected to be $350 billion.
3. MTV is consistently named the top choice for advertisers who want to reach this popular market: "MTV's ability to motivate, influence, entertain, and entice successive generations of young people who have no particular loyalty to any TV entity, or medium itself throughout the social, political,

and cultural changes of two decades, is almost otherworldly" (Ed Martin, *Myers Report*, April 1999). Why? "MTV gives a real intimate way to connect with teens within their familiar environment" (*Mediaweek*, April 19, 1999).

4. MTV's median age is exactly when the majority of young Americans become loyal to brands they are most likely to use for the rest of their lives.

5. People ages twelve to thirty-four accounted for 41 percent of all retail shopping dollars spent in 1998. In fact, twelve- to thirty-four-year-olds spent more money shopping per person than did those over thirty-five. Plus, "Forty-eight percent of young adults have a say in family decisions from paper towels to vacations" (*USA Today*, October 6, 1999).[8]

The two incredibly powerful tools of music and television come together in MTV. The music hooks us, and the visuals reinforce the message of the lyrics in our unprotected mind.

IS THE DEVIL IN THE BEAT?

While attending college, I played drums in a contemporary Christian rock band. We traveled all over California playing at a variety of concerts and events. One Friday night we were scheduled to play at a district-wide youth conference at a Baptist church in Southern California. When we arrived at the church to set up and do a sound check, we were met at the front doors by some of the elders. Almost in unison they said, "You can't bring those demon drums into the holy sanctuary." A few minutes later I found myself sitting behind my drum kit in the hallway, just off stage left of the platform. I guess it was okay for me to play "demon drums" in the hallway of the church, but not the sanctuary!

Many years later, I'm amazed that although that mindset has changed quite a bit, there are still Christians who condemn the use of drums as part of the worship experience in church. There are two main reasons for this kind of attitude. First, it has to do with personal taste. Some people don't like the sound of drums—electronic or acoustic. And because they don't like drums, they don't want them in the church. It's a pretty weak position to force onto everyone else in the church. For example, if I like my steak medium rare and you like yours well done, does that mean that you're wrong and I'm right? Of course not! It just means that we have different tastes in the way we like our meat. And the same could be said about the style of music that we each prefer to listen to.

The second reason for this kind of attitude has to do with a lack of accurate information. Most of the time someone has heard a pastor or speaker make some kind of statement about drums, and they didn't bother to check out the facts for themselves. Again, the Bible makes it very clear that we are to "test everything" (1 Thessalonians 5:21). And this includes what we hear from pastors, speakers, and teachers. Just because someone is on the radio or speaks from a behind a big ol' podium doesn't mean that everything he or she says is accurate, biblically or historically.

Unfortunately, people who take this kind of position about drums try to over-spiritualize things so that no one wants to question them.

Drums in the Bible

The tambourine, a percussion instrument, is mentioned in most Bible translations and comes from the Hebrew word *tof* or *toph,* according to the *New Grove Dictionary of Musical Instruments.* (Some Bible translations use *timbrel* or *tabret.*) The word *toph,* like many names for rhythmic and percussion instruments, is onomatopoeic, which means the name describes its sound. (*Buzz* is another onomatopoeic word.) Other common onomatopoeic names for drums are *conga, tambour, rek, tom-tom, doumbek,* and the word *drum* itself. Each of these names implies a bounce followed by a stop on the drum skin.

Along with cymbals, tambourines appear to be the only percussion instruments listed in the Bible. But the *Oxford Companion of Musical Instruments* makes a distinction about the tambourine mentioned in the Bible; it is more accurately called a *frame drum* and has no metal jingles that we often associate with tambourines we use today. This particular kind of tambourine has a membrane or drum head to strike. These frame drums were commonly used throughout the Middle East in Bible times. Modern tambourines do not usually have a skin or head—except those used in some Latin ensembles—and are often in the shape of a crescent or half circle.

In *Percussion Instruments and Their History,* James Blades makes reference to the instruments of Egypt and Mesopotamia circa 1100 BC. These include frame drums, small kettledrums, and vase-shaped drums made of clay.

Based on this information, we now have a much better idea of what kinds of drums were used in biblical times. But now when we read verses in the Bible that use the word *tambourine,* we really should read it as *frame drum.* In many cultures throughout the world today, frame drums are still popular. They vary in size, and each culture has developed its own playing style of the drum. For example, the Irish *bodhran* is played with a short double-ended stick known as a *tipper.*

Because of the size and portability of frame drums, many women played them in Bible times.

Drumming references in the Bible

The following is a list of places where tambourine ("frame drum") is mentioned in the Bible.

+ Exodus 15:20—"Then Miriam the prophet, Aaron's sister, took a tambourine [drum] and led all the women . . ."
+ 1 Samuel 10:5 NIV—"As you approach the town, you will meet a procession of prophets coming down from the high place with lyres, tambourines [drums] . . ."
+ 1 Samuel 18:6—". . . women from all the towns of Israel came out to meet King Saul. They sang and danced for joy with tambourines [drums] . . ."
+ Psalm 68:25—". . . between them are young women playing tambourines [drums]."
+ Psalm 81:2—"Sing! Beat the tambourine [drum] . . ."
+ Psalm 149:3—"Praise his name with dancing, accompanied by tambourine [drum] . . ."
+ Psalm 150:4—"Praise him with the tambourine [drum] and dancing."
+ Isaiah 30:32—". . . his people will celebrate with tambourines [drums] and harps."

This is not meant to be an exhaustive list of references to drumming in the Bible, but it's obvious that drums appear many times in the Old Testament. There can be no doubt that Miriam and others were actually playing drums in the act of worshiping God.

The beat

While I was being interviewed on a national radio program, a listener called in and asked how I could call myself a Christian and play drums. "Don't you know," she said, "that the beat of rock music is satanic and alters your heartbeat?" As gently as I could (and holding back the laughter as much as possible), I tried to remind this woman that a lot of things alter your heartbeat—running around the block, going on scary rides at an amusement park, or riding a bike. I also tried to help her understand that creation is filled with rhythm. Listen to a bird flapping its wings, the wind rushing through the leaves of a tree, a horse galloping across a field, or even feeling your own pulse. Without a beat, there would be no life.

I've also heard the arguments about the syncopated beat of rock music being erotic and demonic. Or how the drums themselves are sensual because you have to use your entire body to play a drum set. Yes, playing a drum set causes you to move your whole body. It involves four-way coordination between your hands and your feet. You wouldn't be much of a drummer without some movement. By the way, have you ever watched a concert pianist or violinist remain perfectly still while playing his instrument? Of course not!

Drums, whether hand percussion or a drum set, are neither moral nor immoral. They're an instrument—a tool for making music. The real issue becomes how the tool is used. Take a butcher knife, for example. It can be used to cut meat and vegetables, or it can be used to commit murder. Drums can certainly be used to play sensual music, but the same drums can be used to play praise music in church.

This is the core issue when it comes to music being sensual. It's the condition of the heart that we need to look at. The Bible says that as a man "thinks within himself, so he is" (Proverbs 23:7 NIV). In the book of Matthew we read, "For from the heart come evil thoughts, murder, adultery, all sexual immorality, theft, lying, and slander" (15:19). There is no one beat that is more erotic than another; the problem is in your head and your heart. We live in a seductive and sensual society where we're bombarded with sexual images everywhere. Depending upon where your heart and mind are focused, just about any kind of music could be erotic for you.

Drums are a fantastic tool the Lord has given us to boost our worship experience and personal enrichment, and to tell others about His love. Check out your heart and your head—make sure they're right—and leave the rest to God.

How does your music measure up?

To effectively deal with the impact music is having in our lives, we must develop a biblically based strategy (biblical worldview) for evaluating the music we listen to so we can be selective and make better choices. Keep in mind this simple principle: "Garbage in, garbage out." If you feed your mind trash, it's going to come out in your lifestyle. Here are some ideas to get you started.

1. How many hours per day do you spend listening to music? Watching MTV or a similar channel?
2. How much time do you spend reading and studying the Bible each day? In prayer? Remember, listening to praise music is no substitute for spending time in God's Word.
3. Based on your answers to questions 1 and 2, who or what is having the greater influence on your thought life?
4. What does the music you listen to cause you to feel emotionally? What does it cause you to think about? Why do you listen to the groups and artists that you do?
5. Have you ever done something based on what you have listened to or watched on a music video? Be specific (language, hairstyle, clothes, etc.).

6. Ask yourself, *Is what the songwriter wants me to believe or do right for me as a Christian?* Use Philippians 4:8 NIV as a standard for evaluation:

Finally, brothers,
    whatever is true,
    whatever is noble,
    whatever is right,
    whatever is pure,
    whatever is lovely,
    whatever is admirable—
if anything is excellent or praiseworthy—**think** about such things.

Compare the lyrics of a song to this verse and see how they measure up. Don't try to hide behind the excuse that you don't listen to the lyrics, because like it or not, you do. Here's an example. Are you a victim of earworms? It's what happens when an obnoxious song gets stuck in your head. Ninety-eight percent of people surveyed said they were at one time or another bothered by a tune that wouldn't leave their heads. The songs that seem to torment people the most include "YMCA," "We Will Rock You," and "Who Let the Dogs Out?"[9] Just by looking at these titles your brain started replaying the lyrics to these songs. I'd be pretty safe in saying that you never sat down and consciously memorized the lyrics, yet you know them.

It's important to not just to be a sponge and soak everything up. Be selective in the music you listen to. Don't give Satan an avenue into your mind with the tunes of today. Keep evaluating and filtering, using the Bible as your standard. There's also another great resource to help you decide what kind of music to listen to. Check out *www.pluggedinonline.com*. The site is filled with reviews of the latest music, movies, TV shows, and other pop culture stuff.

It may be hard to stop listening to a favorite band or singer, but God will honor your desire to please Him and be obedient. Remember, He wants the best for you and has all the power necessary to help you in this area of your life.

And if you haven't done so already, why not check out some contemporary Christian music? You'll probably be able to find your favorite style of music with positive lyrics. It can really encourage you to grow in your relationship with Jesus.

These are just some of the ways the Enemy attempts to confuse and frustrate us with false teaching related to music. There's no way in a book like this I could mention all the different bands and singers who are in some way linked to the occult or sing empty worldly philosophies. Instead, I've tried to give you some general ideas of what's out there, knowing that new styles and groups appear on the scene frequently. My goal has been to get you to think about what you are putting into your mind by the music you listen to, and to learn to be more discerning.

Think about it

1. What are some of the dangers of being a sponge—just soaking up every message of the music that you listen to?
2. Name one secular song you think a Christian could learn a lot from. Why did you pick that particular song?
3. Suppose you were a parent. What would you tell your kids about what kind of music they should listen to?
4. Is there a band or singer that you need to stop listening to? If so, what are you going to do about it? Remember, you have supernatural resources to help you, and you might also want to find someone to help hold you accountable.

CHAPTER 6

ALTERNATE LIVES

Ever wish that you could be someone else? Maybe you've daydreamed about winning *American Idol* or being a rock star, an MVP athlete, or an Oscar-winning actor. From the time I was a small guy, there were several things I wanted to be when I grew up, including a professional drummer, a policeman, and an actor. Well, I got to live out my alternate life as a drummer for many years (and I still play today). And even my dream to be a cop and an actor were both fulfilled in a low-budget movie shot in Southern California. I spent a day and a half on location at the old Los Angeles County Jail just to film a three-minute segment playing the part of Officer Cavanaugh. I always thought it would have been better to give me an Italian name (hey, when you're Italian, it comes out in everything!), but you can't be real choosy with your first acting gig.

My alternate life for the day was totally cool. Getting fitted for my wardrobe, learning a few lines to say in the movie, hearing the director yell "Action!" and even enjoying the catered meals—all were part of being able to escape reality into a world of fantasy that up until then had been only a dream. I liked it so much that I even asked the director if he could use me in another part. But unfortunately, he said I had such a recognizable face that he couldn't cast me as anyone in the film other than Officer Cavanaugh. I never did figure out if the thing about my face was supposed to be good or bad!

But my fantasy alternate life did become a reality—even if it was for only a day and a half!

A lot of students I meet are looking for alternative lives. They're looking for a way out, a temporary escape from the problems at home and at school. Some are looking for a change, something different, a fantasy life—to escape the boredom of day-to-day existence.

VALUE VS. DANGER

The preferred way of escape is different for each person. Girls have the reputation of being shoppers. Some guys get lost in movies, online, or in TV shows. Other teens read books. Some use illegal drugs or alcohol for the temporary high. Others use sex as their way to break away from the problems of life or boredom. Still other teens become gamers involved in fantasy role-playing games (RPGs), including 16 or 32 multiplayer online games, like Halo. The problem is not in some of the choices for escape (such as reading, shopping, or watching movies), but in the time invested in those activities and the reason behind doing them. If you enjoy reading a good book to relax—great! What an awesome way to engage your mind. But if you're avoiding pain, life, and relationships by filling every gap in time by reading, that can be very unhealthy.

Apply the same concept to RPGs. Unless there's something wrong with the theme of the game (we'll discuss that later), there's nothing wrong with playing a healthy and challenging game to relax and have fun. As you read the next section, don't get me wrong—the issue I'll be talking about isn't fantasy entertainment, it's playing unhealthy role-playing games, or playing them for too many hours or for the wrong reasons.

The problem is that people who get involved with some RPGs find that a little bit of curiosity can lead to an unhealthy fascination and ultimately to an uncontrolled obsession. Sometimes these games can gradually seduce a person mentally and emotionally. Take that a step further, and for many gamers—teens and adults—certain RPGs are the first step into the world of the occult—similar to gateway drugs like marijuana. Gamers can become desensitized to all kinds of evil, violence, and even the occult. Once a player becomes more accepting of evil, Satan slowly sneaks in, using overexposure to evil characters, violence, sex, and occult themes to corrupt values and open minds to his demonic influence and ultimately to destroy.

There's also a danger that some teens and adults can become so consumed by their alternate life, they lose track of what's reality and what's fantasy. Add to this the fact that we live in a society where there are no absolutes and where fantasy and reality are constantly being blurred, and you have big trouble.

Take for example the virtual world of Second Life. It's been described as a game, a tool, a playground, and a nation. According to the Web site, Second Life is a "digital space where everyone can be what they want, create what they want and do what they want."[1] It's a 3D online digital world that is imagined, created, and owned by its residents, who now number over seven million. The Second Life logo symbol is an eye-in-hand or a Talisman—an occultic symbol.

Did you catch on to what you can do in this particular digital world? Your avatar (your persona in the virtual world) can be anything you want it to be. The problem occurs when people go to an extreme to escape reality and find their identity in a digital world. They live in a fantasy world and never effectively deal with the problems they have in the real world. It's easy to lose track of where you are.

A GAME TURNS DEADLY

Take Scott Kammeyer and his two buddies, for example. Scott, Billy Smith, and Joel Henry, all in their upper teens, had been friends for years in their Bakersfield, California, neighborhood, and were heavily involved in the RPG Dungeons & Dragons. Joel was the "master strategist" while Billy and Scott were the "PCs," or "play characters." By the rules of the game, the players are to be completely obedient to the master strategist.

When Joel's family planned to relocate to Texas, he and his buddies devised a way to keep their friendship intact. They decided to kill Scott's parents because they appeared to have more money than anyone else. (They ended up getting the *huge* sum of $185.)

They ambushed Scott's parents after luring them home from work with a lie. At that time, Scott and his two friends imagined they'd shed their real identities and became powerful warriors of destruction. During the slaying, they stayed true to their roles: Joel as master strategist; Scott and Billy acting as play characters.

Each one confessed to the crime when interviewed by detectives. Kern County Sheriff's official Glenn Johnson said the three lived in and out of fantasy and reality so much that they'd finally lost track of where they were. The crime scene was littered with D&D paraphernalia, showing a direct link between the game and the slaying, according to law enforcement authorities.

That's not to say that everyone who plays an RPG is going to end up like Scott Kammeyer and his friends. A game by itself can't make you kill someone or commit a violent act, but it can influence your thinking and desensitize you to certain things. When Scott, Joel, and Billy began playing D&D, they were no different from millions of other kids and adults who get hooked on this popular game. They probably never thought playing an "innocent" game would lead them to murder.

"Stop! Wait a minute, Steve. What about all the stories of people who met online while playing an RPG or multiplayer game and eventually married?" Those are nice, warm, fuzzy stories, but that remote possibility is not a good enough reason to spend multiple hours each day living an alternate life in a fantasy game world.

And remember, it's what we allow inside our hearts and minds that will greatly influence the way we live. As I've said before, the Bible makes it very clear that we are to do whatever we can to guard our minds. Jesus said: "A good person produces good things from the treasury of a good heart, and an evil person produces evil things from the treasury of an evil heart. What you say flows from what is in your heart" (Luke 6:45).

GAMES ON THE DARK SIDE

For as long as there have been computer games, there's been concern about what possible effects they may have on the minds and emotions of kids. A few years ago, *PC Gamer* created a list of the ten most controversial games of all time.[2] Here are the top five from that list:

5. Kingpin
4. Everquest (This multi-player RPG showed up on the controversy map after the highly publicized Thanksgiving 2001 suicide of Shawn Woolley. His mother alleges that Shawn killed himself because he was addicted to EQ.)
3. Panty Raider
2. Postal
1. Doom

Even though we'll probably never see these games as part of a Top Ten list on *Late Show With David Letterman*, there's much we can learn about the potential dangers this kind of entertainment can have on our spiritual lives. And this was hardly a complete listing of games that should cause us to be concerned.

But let's look further, deeper at an even darker side of computer games.

It doesn't take much research on the following list of games to realize how dark the themes and content are: Oogies Revenge; The Thing; American McGee's Alice (a very dark Alice in Wonderland); Clive Barker's Undying; Evil Dead: Regeneration; Evil Islands; Curse of the Lost Soul; Resident Evil series; and Silent Hell: Welcome to Hell. Obviously this list is nowhere near complete, and there have been a bunch of new games developed since I wrote this book. The point is for you to recognize the dark side of the gaming world and start becoming more selective about this part of your entertainment diet. Let's look at a short list of themes and content in these games and others like them.

The themes and content found in these games include:

+ Psychic powers
+ Incantations and spells
+ Violence, gore, and murder
+ Magic and sorcerers
+ Demons
+ The occult
+ Immoral sex
+ Vampires
+ Coarse and foul language
+ Rape and degradation of women

Think about your favorite games and their themes and content. Are they similar to the list above? Are games like these the kind of entertainment you really want to get emotionally and mentally wrapped up in? Do you want this kind of stuff subconsciously influencing the way you think, feel, and act? Look at it this way: How much anthrax does it take to harm you? Just a tiny bit. In other words, it doesn't take much spiritual poison to throw us off track spiritually.

Remember, the list of games is in no way complete. There are plenty of other games on the market just like these, plus there are new ones coming out all the time. And don't forget: Just because I didn't list a specific game in this chapter doesn't mean it's okay to play. Use the principles from the Bible to decide if it's something that God wants you to participate in and allow to influence your thinking.

FinD OTHER OPTiOnS

Even after learning of the dangers of RPGs, some students I've talked to say they have a hard time stopping their involvement with the games. Many tell me they miss the mental stimulation and challenge. I assure them that there's nothing wrong with using your imagination as long as what you are doing is pleasing to God and doesn't violate what the Bible teaches.

Being a Christian doesn't mean you have to be brain-dead or can't use your imagination or that you can't have any fun. No way! It's quite the opposite! I challenge you to get together with your friends and design a fantasy RPG with biblical or historical themes, using intrigue, skill, and wisdom as your weapons to outwit your opponents. (By the way, if you develop a game, let me know so I can share the idea with others!)

The Bible says that we have the mind of Christ (1 Corinthians 2:16). Talk about creative power! We should be the most innovative, cutting-edge people on the planet. The world should be trying to imitate us rather than the other way around. But for that to happen, we have to surrender to Jesus the control of our thought life.

Jesus wants to give us an awesome and meaningful life, better than we ever dreamed possible (John 10:10). And He made it possible for us by dying in our place on the cross and conquering death. So start living and having fun—Jesus' way!

Here are a couple of ideas for alternative ways to challenge yourself mentally. First, if you're into fantasy or sci-fi novels, read books by C. S. Lewis, J. R. R. Tolkien, or up-and-coming authors such as Bryan Davis, Donita Paul, and Karen Hancock—all Christians with incredible imaginations. There are many more quality fantasy/sci-fi books being published. I'm even hoping to write one in the future—so keep an eye out for it!

Second, look for alternative games. Try to find games that are fun, require skill, and challenge you without causing you to compromise biblical values. Again, a good verse to use as a filter, to help you decide what games to play, is Philippians 4:8 NIV: "Finally brothers, whatever is true, whatever is noble, whatever is right, whatever is pure, whatever is lovely, whatever is admirable—if anything is excellent or praiseworthy—think about such things."

Listen up. If you've decided to give up playing a game that's spiritually unhealthy or change your activities online because you realize it's not good for you, it won't be easy. So don't try and do it alone. Begin by asking God in prayer for help and strength. Then go to a parent, youth pastor, or another Christian adult you trust and tell him or her about your decision. That person can keep you accountable and be a real source of encouragement as well as answer any questions you may have.

THE DARK SIDE OF THE NET

Another place where it's easy to live out an alternate life is online. The Net is an awesome tool—for good and for evil. It's incredible how much information we now have available to us in just a few seconds. You can find out information about rare diseases. You can read an entire book. You can develop a relationship in a chat room. Or you can even IM someone halfway around the world, having a written conversation that only a few years ago would have taken weeks through the mail system.

The scariest part is that it is also easy to access information about all sorts of evil, occult activities, and witchcraft online. It doesn't take much to seduce you into places where you have no business being as a child of God. While it may seem harmless and innocent, curiosity can trip you up and lead you to a place you don't want to go.

There's a place online called "The Dark Side of the Net—bringing you into the darkness since 1993." It's like a central location for all kinds of dark links, including news, special events, convergences, haunted houses, and resources. There are links to dark literature, art, entertainment, chat rooms, music, movies, and of course games—card, paper, board, and computer.

Look at the whole porn craze. You don't even have to go looking for this stuff. It will pop up on your screen or be disguised in a spam message that can bait your curiosity. It is easy to become addicted to porn or other sorts of evil. Pastors are not immune—some have become addicted to online porn themselves.

If you're not careful, cyberspace can be a very dangerous place. Not only is it addictive, but you can also easily lose yourself online for hours. It's easy to be subtly seduced with empty values and beliefs. In the New Testament, Paul writes to a young leader named Timothy, warning him about this very thing: "Timothy, guard what God has entrusted to you. Avoid godless, foolish discussions with those who oppose you with their so-called knowledge. Some people have wandered from the faith by following such foolishness" (1 Timothy 6:20–21).

WHAT THE BIBLE HAS TO SAY

If you're determined to grow in your relationship with Jesus and want the very best He has to offer, then you need to take the Bible so seriously that you will practice obeying it in every dimension of your life, including entertainment and recreation. It's important to develop a biblical worldview that can act as a filter in your life.

To help you do this, let's check out what the Bible says about some of the content and themes in certain chat rooms, message boards, and Web sites on the Internet. Then make your decision about the games based on the standards of God's Word.

Evil

+ "Don't get sidetracked; keep your feet from following evil" (Proverbs 4:27).
+ "Since they thought it foolish to acknowledge God, he abandoned them to their foolish thinking and let them do things that should never be done. Their lives became full of every kind of wickedness, sin, greed, hate, envy, murder, quarreling, deception, malicious behavior, and gossip. They are backstabbers, haters of God, insolent, proud, and boastful. They invent new ways of sinning, and they disobey their parents. They refuse to understand, break their promises, are heartless, and have no mercy. They know God's justice requires that those who do these things deserve to die, yet they do them anyway. Worse yet, they encourage others to do them, too" (Romans 1:28–32).
+ "Dear friend, don't let this bad example influence you. Follow only what is good. Remember that those who do good prove that they are God's children, and those who

do evil prove that they do not know God" (3 John 11).

God has a plan and purpose for each one of us. He has a road of life that will give us the greatest amount of happiness and satisfaction. But that means we need to stay on God's pathway and not get sidetracked on detours, including evil in any form. God feels so strongly about the hazards of evil that He doesn't even want us to imitate it.

Magic, spells, and sorcery

+ "Never sacrifice your son or daughter as a burnt offering. And do not let your people practice fortune-telling, or use sorcery, or interpret omens, or engage in witchcraft, or cast spells, or function as mediums or psychics, or call forth the spirits of the dead" (Deuteronomy 18:10–11).
+ "Blessed are those who wash their robes. They will be permitted to enter through the gates of the city and eat the fruit from the tree of life. Outside the city are the dogs—the sorcerers, the sexually immoral, the murderers, the idol worshipers, and all who love to live a lie" (Revelation 22:14–15).

The Bible leaves no room for doubt where God stands on the use of magic, spells, or sorcery of any form. He wants us to have nothing to do with them. Why? Because they are harmful to us, especially when it comes to entertainment. When we're having "fun" doing something, it's easy to ignore the potential dangers. Remember, God is for you and always wants the best for you. He demonstrated this total love to us in a way no one else ever could—by the death of His only Son Jesus on the cross.

Immorality and sex

+ "Run from sexual sin! No other sin so clearly affects the

body as this one does. For sexual immorality is a sin against your own body" (1 Corinthians 6:18).

+ "Let there be no sexual immorality, impurity, or greed among you. Such sins have no place among God's people" (Ephesians 5:3).

+ "So put to death the sinful, earthly things lurking within you. Have nothing to do with sexual immorality, impurity, lust, and evil desires. Don't be greedy, for a greedy person is an idolater, worshiping the things of this world" (Colossians 3:5).

Coarse language and swearing

+ "Obscene stories, foolish talk, and coarse jokes—these are not for you. Instead, let there be thankfulness to God" (Ephesians 5:4).

+ "But now is the time to get rid of anger, rage, malicious behavior, slander, and dirty language" (Colossians 3:8).

Murder and violence

+ "You must not murder" (Exodus 20:13).

+ "You have heard that our ancestors were told, 'You must not murder. If you commit murder, you are subject to judgment'"(Matthew 5:21).

+ "Wise words will win you a good meal, but treacherous people have an appetite for violence" (Proverbs 13:2).

+ "The Lord examines both the righteous and the wicked. He hates those who love violence" (Psalm 11:5).

+ "Don't let liars prosper here in our land. Cause great disasters to fall on the violent" (Psalm 140:11).

RPGs not only influence our thinking, but they also have the potential to cause havoc in our lives. Remember, it's important to guard against overexposing our minds to evil philosophies and themes.

It will be difficult letting go of something that has been consuming vast amounts of your time and energy, but it's like dealing with any other habit that needs to be broken: Take it one day at a time. Avoid putting unrealistic expectations on yourself. But also be careful not to procrastinate.

All the resources of heaven are available to you to help you win in this dimension of your life. Take the first step toward change and God will help you to do the rest!

THINK ABOUT IT

1. Read James 1:8. How does this verse apply to a Christian involved with unhealthy games or Internet sites?
2. How can you tell the difference between fantasy and reality?
3. What does it mean to participate in a game (or anything else) that glorifies evil? (Start by looking up the definition of *participate*.)
4. What would be the best way to help a family member or friend who is addicted to an unhealthy game or online site recognize the dangers?

CHAPTER 7

PAGANISM, WICCA, AND WITCHCRAFT

Ed was raised in a Southern Baptist church. As a teenager he was involved in the youth group and a variety of evangelism projects. But by the time he graduated from high school, he was finished with church and God. Ed said he could not find the answers he was looking for about life and didn't like hearing about the wars Christians had started and how intolerant they were.

In his late twenties he met a man who totally changed his spiritual dimension by introducing him to Wicca. For the first time, Ed felt like he finally had some answers about spirituality—and life. Eventually Ed and this man would start the Witch School in Illinois. The Witch School now boasts over 186,000 registered students online and is said to be the first online school dedicated to Wiccan, pagan, and magickal thought. Students can enroll in a variety of courses including Séance 101, Basic Spell Writing, Basics of Voodoo, Five Mystic Secrets, Crystal and Gem Magic, Divination, Zombies, Psychic Development, and Living the Wiccan Life.

✝ ✝ ✝

Laurie Cabot, the seventy-four-year-old official witch of Salem, Massachusetts, is an ordained High Priestess descended from Celtic ancestry. She is one of millions of witches worldwide and says witchcraft is an earth-based religion with heavy environmental overtones. According to Cabot, witches are not Satanists and don't believe in evil, Satan, or sacrificing animals. Doing evil is supposedly against one of the basic principles of their religion; if you do anything bad, it comes back to you three times. Any magic witches do is "for the good of all," as they say at the end of spells.[1]

✝ ✝ ✝

Kaytee, a sixteen-year-old high school junior who wants to be an actress, is a witch. So are her mother, her father, and her eight-year-old sister. Kaytee's parents are first-degree witches, but Kaytee is still practicing for initiation. She's learning the basics of alpha and about the god and goddesses of the magick circle. Everyone at her school knows she's into witchcraft, although most don't understand it.

Kaytee says she is going to use her first spell to help her get the part of Peter Pan in the school play. "It's like prayer," she says. "I will project that I will get this part of Peter Pan in the musical, 'harm me none and for the good of all.'"[2]

✝ ✝ ✝

Paganism, Wicca, and witchcraft are popular ways of exploring spirituality today. The "dark side" of spirituality is especially appealing with teens. A lot of students I meet are disillusioned with the organized church and are disappointed with God because they feel like He has somehow abandoned them. They have turned to a form of paganism where they feel their needs are being met and where they have the power to handle the challenges of life. But trying to understand the difference between paganism, Wicca, and witchcraft can be a little confusing.

Paganism is hundreds of things mixed together, including the worship of nature, the Norse god, Egyptian gods, Native American and Australian Aborigine Shamanism, Wicca, witchcraft, voodoo, African native religions, and too many others to list.

Witchcraft is the "craft in the sense of the art or skill of a practicing pagan."[3] It is the worship of nature and the practice of magick.

Wicca is a subset of paganism. The word was first used about fifty years ago to define a religion built from what was thought to have been practiced in ancient times, which includes a belief in the god and goddess, honoring the Rede ("Harm no one, do what you will") and the Rule of Three or the Threefold Law ("Anything you do will come back to you three times over"), and celebrating the Wheel of the Year (days of power on the calendar).

I've heard some involved in this dark side of spirituality explain the differences in this way: Most witches are pagans, but not all pagans are witches; not all witches are Wiccans; and a witch who practices witchcraft does not necessarily believe in the religion of Wicca. Are you confused yet? You're not alone—even those who practice one of these forms of spirituality are not necessarily fully informed. Wicca is the most popular and common practice of the three today. It has great appeal among teens and is referred to as the fastest-growing religion among high school and college students in North America. So let's take a quick look at Wicca as a contemporary expression of paganism and witchcraft.

WHAT'S THE APPEAL?

Wicca is basically a self-styled religion—it gives you the freedom to believe in whatever you want—and it is this concept that is by far the most appealing thing about Wicca. But there are many other things that make Wicca appealing, including:

+ *Tolerance.* Many teens are turned off by what they view as discrimination from conservative Christian churches on things like sexual orientation, religious beliefs, and marital status.

+ *Environmental consciousness.* Wiccans have strong beliefs regarding respect and care for the earth and all species of plants and animals. Wiccans are very connected to the earth and cycles of nature. They get their theology from nature and completely reject the biblical principle about humans being masters over fish, birds, and animals (Genesis 1:28). They believe we should live in complete cooperation with nature.

+ *"Whatever" experience.* Some teens don't like the way church is practiced today. They see it as too much of a spectator event. They want more direct participation—experience. With Wicca they can not only perform rituals solo or in a group (coven), they can design their own. Rituals can be performed any place at any time. Everything is totally up to them—what they believe and what they do.

+ *Sexual equality.* In most Wiccan traditions, equality between the sexes is a common principle. Wiccans believe men and women have both a male and a female side and a responsibility to balance the two. Most believe the female principle is very powerful—and most of the time more important than the male. This is very appealing to teens who reject what they believe is male domination in the church.

+ *Power.* Probably one of the initial attractions for teens is power. They desire to feel special and sometimes to get vengeance on others who have hurt them. They also desire to gain control over their lives through spells, incantations, and other mystical tools like rocks and crystals.

+ *Personal control.* Wicca is very personal in the way it's practiced. You could ask ten self-professed Wiccans to explain the religion, and you'd hear fifty different responses. It's hugely appealing when you can pick and choose what you want to believe. You come up with your own version of Wicca and what works best for you. Wicca also offers the opportunity to design your own deities (gods).

People like Ed, Laurie, and Kaytee want us to think that paganism, Wicca, and witchcraft will provide all the answers about this life and the next. But before we buy in to what they've decided to live by, maybe we better find out what they believe and what God thinks about these beliefs. Because Wicca has the biggest following, we'll focus on the Wiccan religion and what they believe.

WHAT WITCHES BELIEVE

In my book *What's the Deal With Wicca,* I go into great detail on what those who practice Wicca believe. For the sake of space in this book, we will take a look at only some of the basics. If you'd like to learn more, check out *What's the Deal With Wicca.*

Wicca is a very individualistic and experiential religion, with a lot of emphasis on personal responsibility. For example, in Wicca, there's no need to confess sin and receive forgiveness from an outside "authority." Instead you're supposed to own up to your actions, admit your mistakes, and make things right wherever you can. Wiccans do not believe in the concept of absolute evil or the existence of Satan. They also do not believe in God, but in themselves as gods: "We owe no allegiance to any person or power greater than the Divinity manifest through our own being."[4] They believe that anything you do—good or bad—will return to you three times over. Most Wiccans don't submit to any centralized authority, and they're against any organized belief system. Instead they build their own religion by mixing and matching various views and practices. Wicca, like other neopagan religions, draws heavily on experience, so truth is relative. They're convinced that the only way you can know truth is through a sixth sense or feelings. There are no absolutes. But there are some basic beliefs that are held sacred by all Wiccans, out of which come the individual practices and traditions.

Wicca is a religion built around worship of two deities: the goddess and the god. Before the creation of the earth, the "All" existed. This female spirit was alone, so she created her other half—the male spirit. And even though they were two spirits, they were one, and they gave birth to the universe. They made the stars, moons, solar system, and planets. While on the earth they made water, land, plants, animals, and people.

The All—equally female and male—created the seeds of life. The god and goddess chose the sun and the moon to remind us of their presence. The sun is the physical symbol for the god, and the moon is the physical symbol for the goddess. The goddess is the female force, the portion of the ultimate energy source that created the universe. She is all-woman, all-fertility, all-love.[5] The god is the male force, the other half of the primal divine energy acknowledged by Wiccans. He is all-man, all-fertility, all-love.[6]

Wicca is grounded in the worship of the earth, which is seen as an expression of the "mother goddess" and her companion "the horned god." Both of these deities manifest themselves in nature. Wiccans see the earth as a living goddess who blesses us and must be nurtured and cared for in return.[7] They believe that the goddess dwells in every single thing—in trees, rocks, raindrops, and even inside of you. In many ways, Wicca is similar to the nature religions mentioned in the Bible, where many gods were worshiped and religions mixed, like the fertility religions of Canaan (1 Kings 14:22–24).[8]

In Wicca you choose the form of deity that you work with, based on your personal preferences and what you want to work on. You can choose from lots of different gods and goddesses and traditions. Naming a god is all about choosing what works for you based on the things that you identify with, relate to, like, and love. You have the complete freedom to choose whatever god you want to worship. Plus, you work *with* your deities rather than beg for help *from* them.

The "Days of Power"—the sacred holidays that make up the Wiccan calendar—come from the earliest observances of seasons and cycles. In the craft, it is called the Wheel of the Year. The image of an ever-turning wheel is symbolic of the Wiccan view of life: the constancy of change, the flow of season into season, and humankind's inseparable relationship with the earth.[9]

Wiccans celebrate eight main holidays or *Sabbats*. They are all centered on the solar cycles and occur at the time of natural events associated with the change of seasons. At least once per month witches also celebrate an esbat—a Wiccan moon ritual when the goddess is honored. An esbat can be celebrated on a full moon or on any other phase of the moon. They are times to draw on your energy and do magick.

Most Wiccans begin their year on October 31 with *Samhain*. On this night they revere their friends and loved ones who have passed on to the other life. They also mark the symbolic death of the god on this night. This day is linked with the coming of winter. *Yule* is celebrated around December 21 (the date changes each year because of the solstices and equinoxes). On this day the rebirth of the god through the action of the goddess is celebrated.

Wiccans celebrate the recovery of the goddess from giving birth to the god on *Imbolc* (February 1 or 2). It's a festival for the renewing fertility of the earth. *Ostara*—the spring solstice—is celebrated on or around March 21. It marks the first day of spring and the time of awakening of the goddess (earth) as the sun grows in warmth and power. April 30 is called *Beltane,* and it is the festival to recognize the young god venturing into manhood. He and the goddess—now his lover instead of his mother—fall in love and unite, producing the bounty of nature.

Wiccans believe in reincarnation, which deepens their need to learn from all experiences. There's no actual heaven or hell, but instead they believe in a place called Summerland, where they go after dying to wait for a new physical form. This is a place where the spirit goes to think about the life it just lived, what it learned, and where it will come back next. If a soul doesn't want to reincarnate right away, it can become a spirit guide. Ultimately, once a spirit has learned all it's supposed to learn and perfected this knowledge, it will be reunited and absorbed into the All.

Spell-casting and magick are a vital part of Wicca. Spells are seen as symbolic acts performed in an altered state of consciousness in order to cause a desired change. Spell-casting is a form of visualization also known as "guided imagery" or "mind over matter." *The Teen Spell Book* says that spells and tools of the craft are only as powerful as the emotions they raise inside of you.[10]

A basic sacred text for many witches is something they call a Book of Shadows (grimoire). It's called a Book of Shadows because magick works outside of time and space and in the "in-between" space of light and darkness, sounds and silences—the shadows. Plus, in the past, witches would have to gather for their celebrations or exchange information in the shadows. A Book of Shadows is a spiritual diary that contains spells, spiritual thoughts, and formulas for the proper preparation of potions. Anything and everything related to your craft experience can be put in your Book of Shadows. It's like a personal reference book.

It all sounds pretty appealing. But the big problem is that Wiccans are trying to live life completely independent of God. Witchcraft is self-centered and encourages you to depend on yourself and the power within you. The God of Creation, who made you and me, says, "Apart from me you can do nothing" (John 15:5).

WHAT GOD THINKS

Wicca, paganism, and witchcraft are huge with students today. But before you start thinking they're cool, let's see what the Bible has to say.

Both the Old and the New Testaments make repeated references to the practice of witchcraft and sorcery. In every instance where these practices are mentioned, God condemns them. The Bible condemns all forms of witchcraft, including sorcery, astrology, and magic.

God is so concerned about this subject that He very specifically warns us in His Word to stay away from it. In the book of 2 Chronicles, we read the story about a man named Manasseh who became a king at the ripe old age of twelve. He did evil in the eyes of the Lord and paid a huge price for his bad choices. Here's what God said about Manasseh's involvement in witchcraft:

Manasseh also sacrificed his own sons in the fire in the valley
of Ben-Hinnom. He practiced sorcery, divination, and witchcraft, and he consulted with mediums and psychics. He did
much that was evil in the Lord's sight, arousing his anger.
(2 Chronicles 33:6)

Just because this story is about a king who lived a few thousand years ago doesn't mean that God has changed His mind
about witchcraft. This warning is just as relevant to us as it was
to previous generations. Provoking God to anger is not a very
smart thing to do. Why would God get angry about this kind of
practice? Because He wants us to rely on *Him* for guidance,
power, and direction. He is our strength and our life; the forces
of darkness are not.

God uses the Old Testament prophet Micah to warn the Isra-
elites about going to witches for answers about life: "I will put
an end to all witchcraft, and there will be no more fortune-
tellers" (Micah 5:12).

In the New Testament book of Galatians, the apostle Paul
warns us to beware of the strong pull of our sinful nature that
can cause us to rebel against God and sin. Let's look at Galatians
5:19–21:

When you follow the desires of your sinful nature, the results
are very clear: sexual immorality, impurity, lustful pleasures, idol-
atry, sorcery, hostility, quarreling, jealousy, outbursts of anger,
selfish ambition, dissension, division, envy, drunkenness, wild
parties, and other sins like these. Let me tell you again, as I have
before, that anyone living that sort of life will not inherit the
Kingdom of God.

What an ugly list of sins witchcraft has been included in!
Carefully consider Paul's warning at the end of this passage
regarding the kingdom of God.

The Bible makes it very clear that Jesus is the only way to get to God and ultimately heaven. He is also the key to life on this planet (John 14:6). Did you notice that Wiccans not only talk very little about life after death, but they also don't have a solution for the problem of sin and guilt?

WATCHING OUT FOR WITCHCRAFT

As Christians, we need to be prepared to respond to the influence of witchcraft. Things associated with witchcraft can show up in a variety of ways in many different places.

You don't have to look very hard to find examples of the influence of Wicca, paganism, and witchcraft on TV. *Ghost Whisperer* is about a young newlywed with a unique ability to communicate with the earthbound spirits of people who have died and need her help. In *Supernatural,* brothers Sam and Dean Winchester are on a dangerous other-worldly mission. In their '67 Chevy Impala, they travel on mysterious back roads of the country hunting down evil supernatural forces they encounter. Still around in reruns is *Charmed,* which is about three young and beautiful women who just happen to be witches. And don't forget the ever-present *Sabrina, the Teenage Witch* and *Buffy the Vampire Slayer.*

Think about the movies you see. Not all movies are bad, but some do promote the principles of witchcraft. Take for example the film *Ghost Rider.* Johnny Blaze is a young stunt cyclist who sells his soul to the demonic Mephistopheles in order to save his dying father. The cost of selling his soul comes back to haunt him years later when he eventually becomes Ghost Rider—a supernatural agent of vengeance.

Millions have read and watched the adventures of Harry Potter and his friends. The storylines aren't very subtle at the Hogwarts School of Witchcraft and Wizardry. It's been interesting to watch the evolution of this series as it has gotten progressively darker and more violent. While doing research for my book on Wicca, I happened on a store in northern California where Harry Potter had come alive. It wasn't just trinkets and memorabilia but rather all the actual stuff from *Harry Potter*—the real deal for real witchcraft.

The Craft has become a modern witchcraft classic. Some say it's a "chick" version of a classic vampire flick. *The Craft* features the most beautiful witches in history as well as a series of teen struggles that are solved by the creative use of magick. Or how about the dark and violent movies like the *Saw* series, *Texas Chainsaw Massacre* series, or the *Hostel* flicks. There seems to be a hunger for darkness and violence as we have become more desensitized to evil in our culture.

Obviously I couldn't list everything that is on the screen today, but we've briefly looked at a sample of what's out there that is evil, scary, and magical all at the same time. Unfortunately, it can confuse us as to the response God wants us to have toward witchcraft. We need to realize that unless we've put our faith and trust in Jesus, we don't have the power within us to deal with the challenges of life.

Satan has an impressive way of making witchcraft look fashionable and appealing. Stevie Nicks, the female lead singer of the mega-selling rock band Fleetwood Mac, is a self-avowed white witch.[11] She and the band performed years ago in a reunion concert at one of the parties celebrating the inauguration of President Bill Clinton. When a witch is performing at that level, it can deceive you into thinking that witchcraft can't be all that bad.

Witchcraft and its influences can also be found in your computer games, board games, and comic books. And there's even the influence of witchcraft in the environmental movement.

There has never been a generation so environmentally conscious as today's. And among those encouraging us to "be nice to mother earth," witches are at the front of the line.

While we need to do our part in being environmentally sensitive, we also need to be careful not to get things out of balance. God has called us to be caretakers of the planet. In Genesis 2:15 we read, "The Lord God placed the man in the Garden of Eden to tend and watch over it." But the Bible also teaches us that we are to worship the Creator, not the creation. In Exodus 20:3 NIV God says, "You shall have no other gods before me." While those practicing witchcraft may be helping the environment, they go about it in the wrong way, looking to self for the power to invoke change. Remember to keep your eyes and heart centered on God as you strive to do the right thing.

Mattel toys even got into the witchcraft act a few years ago with the "Secret Spells Barbie." Ads for the doll said that it could help you get luck, money, and love. Strange, huh?

GOING TO THE RIGHT SOURCE

While on vacation in Massachusetts I decided to visit the town of Salem. It's a beautiful area and a fascinating town. Just about everywhere I went I saw a black symbol of a witch riding a broomstick. It was on store windows and in publications—almost like a town logo. At the Salem Witch Museum, your tour begins by showing you a vivid reenactment of the witch trials of 1692. You walk away wondering how things got so out of control. Then you are encouraged to tour the rest of the museum at your own pace. This part was basically a huge commercial for Wicca and witchcraft. As I left the museum I noticed something very interesting. When you first approach the museum, it looks like an ancient dark haunted gothic castle. But when you look

down the side of the building you see a modern well-kept struc-
ture. The gothic castle part of the building is a false front much
like you would find on a studio back lot. What a vivid reminder
of the deceptive path the devil tries to lead us down.

Maybe you've been able to take a firm stand when it comes
to things like Wicca, but what if a good friend starts to show an
interest in magic spells? How should you respond? Start by praying and asking God to help you find out why your friend would
be interested in witchcraft. Sometimes people start playing
around with this stuff at parties out of curiosity. They want to
see if there's really any power that can be gained. Dabbling like
this can be dangerous; it can be a gateway to the occult and
Satanism.

For others, becoming involved with witchcraft comes from a
sincere search for power to change their life or to deal with the
pain of a broken home, rejection, or hopelessness. While witchcraft may appear to offer immediate power for change, it's temporary and limited at best. It also leaves God totally out of the
picture and relies on power from the forces of darkness.

The power that we need to handle the pressures of life is
found in the resurrection of Jesus Christ. The same power that
God used to bring Jesus back to life after being in the grave for
three days is available to help us overcome all the challenges and
issues in our daily life. And it's unlimited power!

The best way to apply this power is through prayer. When
you or someone you care about is facing tough times, ask God
for His strength and wisdom to face the situation. Put your
energy and effort into prayerfully seeking God's help and
answers. Also make sure you're getting a steady diet of answers
from God's Word. The Bible is God's handbook for living, and
it contains supernatural guidance that only God can give.

Don't fall into the trap of quick, "microwavable" answers

gained from chants and spells. Go to the Author of life itself, and trust God, even though sometimes it seems He takes a long time to answer. The Bible says in 2 Peter 3:8–9: "You must not forget this one thing, dear friends: A day is like a thousand years to the Lord, and a thousand years is like a day. The Lord isn't really being slow about his promise, as some people think. No, he is being patient for your sake. He does not want anyone to be destroyed, but wants everyone to repent." God's answer is always perfect no matter how long you have to wait for it.

Satan will do anything to sugarcoat evil, making it easier to seduce us away from our family, church, and God. Don't be confused by people like Ed, Laurie Cabot, and others who sprinkle bits of truth in with the lies. It's okay to be concerned about the environment, equal treatment of the sexes, and other things that are important to God as well as to our society. Do your part in making positive changes. But always take your stand based on the absolute truth of God's Word. Make sure you are living your life for and like Jesus—then you'll have the answers, courage, and power to respond to the challenges of life.

THINK ABOUT IT

1. There are many places in the Bible where God addresses the subject of witchcraft. Check out what God says in each passage and what our response should be as Christians:
   - Deuteronomy 18:9–13
   - Nahum 3:4
   - 2 Kings 9:22
   - Micah 5:12
   - Revelation 21:8

   Is witchcraft really "positive, harmless, and empowering"?

2. Many books, TV shows, and movies that include witch-craft and sorcery are accepted by some Christians. Does the fact that a book, movie, or TV show involving witch-craft necessarily mean we should not read or watch it? If so, why? If not, how should we decide?

3. What is one way you can personally respond to the problems with the environment in a way that honors God? When, where, and with whom do you need to accomplish this action?

4. Do you have a friend or family member who is messing around with witchcraft? Besides praying for this person, how else does God want you to respond and help him or her?

CHAPTER 8

SATANISM, NEW AGE, AND THE OCCULT

Justin wanted to talk about spirituality and his religion. He was a practicing Satanist. He wanted to make sure I knew that Satanism isn't about taking drugs, and it isn't about harming little kids or pets. "Satanism respects and exalts life," he said. "Uniqueness and creativity are encouraged, not mindless conformity."

Justin went on to explain that Satanists believe good and evil are merely terms that some people twist to suit their own purposes. And in the end, each person must make the final judgment about right and wrong. For them, Satan is a symbol of the power of that choice. Justin said what really matters is that you're a mature, sensitive, self-aware individual who revels in the darkness and who wants to connect with others who believe the same way. "A Satanist challenges that which is presumed to be true," he said. Confident that he had made his case with me, Justin walked off into the night.

In his mind I'm sure he felt like he had a good grasp of Satanism, but I'm not so sure he fully understood what he was ultimately involved in. Justin's like a lot of teenagers I meet who are exploring spirituality and looking for freedom to preserve true individuality and creativity.

In this chapter we'll be taking a closer look at three specific directions some students turn to in their search: Satanism, New Age, and the occult.

What is Satanism?

Most of the time you'd have a hard time picking a Satanist out of the crowd. There's no certain way Satanists dress, although sometimes they do wear black cloaks and pentacles. They work out in the gym, listen to music—gothic, black metal, classical, classic rock—and even work at some pretty ordinary jobs. But it's what they believe that sets them apart.

Defining *Satanism* is no easy task. One Web site says it has been called the "unreligion" because it does not subscribe to the notion of a deity with human form or attributes, nor a being who must be worshiped.

For Satanists, Satan is considered the prototype or original pattern to be followed. Basically, Satan represents certain qualities that the Satanist embodies—for example, the questioning of all, avoiding oppressive thinking, determination toward success and human potential, and a rational self-interest. Satanism embraces numerous cultural and religious ideas and concepts from ancient Rome, Egypt, and Greece, as well as elements from Zoroastrianism, Hinduism, and a lot of other belief systems. Basically, a Satanist accepts Satan as a life principle worth following.

Even though Satanists are free to choose how and what characteristics of Satan they will imitate, most would agree to follow the "Nine Satanic Statements." These often directly oppose what God says to do. For example, they are encouraged to indulge rather than abstain. They give kindness only to those who deserve it—unlike Christ, who gives grace to all whether they deserve it or not. The statements encourage vengeance and indulging in all sins for the sake of self-gratification. They see men as just another animal, not as a special, unique creation of God.

There are also "Eleven Satanic Rules of the Earth," which are important guidelines for the Satanist to pursue. The frightening thing about these rules is that they begin with a statement that sounds great, like, "When in another's lair, show him respect or else do not go there." However, "If a guest in your lair annoys you, treat him cruelly and without mercy." The rules encourage using magick to "successfully obtain your desires." They allow for individual decisions about sex, stealing, and deciding whether or not to destroy someone.

Satanists have an interesting and a confusing way of thinking. First they say they don't believe in Satan. But Satan is the one they are trying to imitate and the one they want to follow. It doesn't make much sense.

You can also frequently hear them say this phrase: "Hail, Satan!" It can be interpreted in two ways. First, it's a type of acknowledgment of Satan's achievements, his heritage, and character. But it's also another way of saying, "Hail, me!" since Satanists imitate the qualities of the devil himself, who began the lie that we can be the "god" of our world and should live independent of God.

Remember, Satan is really at the heart of Satanism. Since we already covered what the Bible says about Satan in chapter 3 ("Do You Know Your Enemy?"), I won't repeat the same information here. But if you feel like you need a quick review, go back over that chapter. It might just help you get a better understanding of Satanism.

Now let's take a closer look at another weapon in the devil's arsenal—New Age—and how it fits into Satan's overall strategy to deceive and mislead.

WHAT IS NEW AGE?

Time magazine calls New Age "a combination of spirituality and superstition, fad and force, about which the only thing certain is that it is not new."[1] Essentially, New Age is nothing but ancient Hinduism and occultism repackaged. Leaders within the movement say it is amazing what you can get people to do when you take away the Hindu and occult terminology and use contemporary language.

New Age can be defined as the penetration of Eastern and occult mysticism into Western culture. The term *New Age* refers to the Aquarian Age, which some New Agers believe is dawning, bringing with it an era of enlightenment, peace, prosperity, and perfection. That's exactly what Satan would like us to think! In reality, the New Age movement is simply opening the doors to his destructive influence in our culture even wider than before.

New Age is another weapon in the devil's arsenal to lure us away from God's truth. The following statistics give us a brief glimpse of the progress Satan is making in shaping the thinking of teens.

+ 35 percent of teens said that they "have personally experienced something that could only be explained by supernatural or spiritual reasons."
+ 30 percent of teens said they have personally encountered an angel, demon, or some other supernatural being.
+ 10 percent of teens said they have communicated with the dead.
+ 13 percent of teens claimed they know someone who has psychic powers.
+ 7 percent of teens said they believe they personally have psychic powers.
+ 79 percent of teens have looked at their horoscope.
+ 82 percent of teens said they have been exposed to the supernatural world through media in the last three months (TV, books, movies, etc.)

+ 73 percent of teens said they had personally engaged in at least one type of psychic or witchcraft-related activity during their life.[2]

It's amazing how popular New Age has become. You can go into almost any bookstore and find a massive section of books relating to various aspects of New Age. Entire magazines are devoted to it.

New Age concepts have also been steadily introduced and made popular by a variety of celebrities like actress Shirley MacLaine; TV psychic John Edward, host of the cable show *Cross Country*; David Carradine; Richard Gere; Tom Cruise; and John Travolta.

Another example of a New Age celebrity is guru and bestselling author Deepak Chopra. *Time* magazine calls him the "poet-prophet of alternative medicine." Chopra believes people can become one with anything: "If you're in unity consciousness, the whole world is animated to you. You can talk to trees and stars. Everything is part of your body."[3] Don't forget infomercial self-help guru Tony Robbins, who helps people "unleash the power within."

New Age and occult themes can be found in movies and TV series like the *Star Wars* saga and the *Star Trek* series. *Peaceful Warrior* is billed as a film about the power of the human spirit. It's a true story based on Dan Millman's bestselling novel. The story is about a gifted young athlete who has it all—including a shot at the Olympics. But after a life-changing accident, Dan comes to rely on a mysterious stranger names Socrates and an elusive young woman named Joy, who teach him the secret to overcome odds and tap in to new worlds of strength and understanding.

There are also Eastern religions and New Age elements

found in movies such as *Atlantis: The Lost Empire, Dragonfly, Bulletproof Monk, Final Fantasy: The Spirits Within, Jack Frost, The Medallion,* and *Spirited Away.* New Age products and gadgets seem to be flooding the marketplace: singing Tibetan bowls, crystals, pyramids, tarot cards, charms, fortune-telling devices, computer software, and even "rebirthing" tanks.

New Age and occult elements are also found in the work of some popular music artists. Here are some examples:

+ India.Arie, *Acoustic Soul* and *Voyage to India*
+ Live, *Secret Samadhi*
+ Madonna, *American Life*
+ Sarah McLachlan, *Surfacing*
+ Pearl Jam, *Riot Act* and *No Code*
+ Sting, *Brand New Day*

The New Age movement has become more than a fad. It's a lifestyle for many. From the outside, the New Age movement is very appealing. It's trying to accomplish some good things. For example, they want to take care of the homeless and eliminate all disease and racial tension in the world. And they're very concerned about the environment.

But most likely the biggest appeal of New Age is that you can be your own god. And that's the same desire that got Satan kicked out of heaven in the first place (Isaiah 14:12–14).

SIX PRINCIPLES OF ПEW AGE THINKING

The following principles form the "revolutionary understanding" shared by those involved in the movement. As you will see, each one of these principles is a clever, subtle counterfeit of biblical Christianity.

All is one. One is all. (monism)

According to New Age beliefs, every little particle in the universe and every piece of matter everywhere is interconnected, all made of the same "stuff." Everything swims in this huge cosmic interconnected ocean. There's no difference between rocks, trees, humans, animals, and God. We are all the same. The reason we have problems in our world today is not because of evil, but ignorance. We are ignorant of the fact that we are all interconnected.

The Bible teaches something entirely different in Colossians 1:16–17:

> For through him [Christ] God created everything in the heavenly realms and on earth. He made the things we can see and the things we can't see—such as thrones, kingdoms, rulers, and authorities in the unseen world. Everything was created through him and for him. He existed before anything else, and he holds all creation together.

God is separate from His creation. The Bible also tells us that we are separated from God because of our sin (Romans 3:23). In New Age teaching there is no need for forgiveness, since we are all one vast interconnected ocean.

God is everything. Everything is God. (pantheism)

New-Agers say that everything in creation is part of God: trees, snails, people, etc. Everything has a divine, godlike nature. It is part of God. The idea of a personal God needs to be abandoned. You don't need a savior because you are part of God. If God (he or she) does exist at all, "it" really just started a "Big Bang" many years ago and is now just an impersonal force floating around in the cosmos somewhere.

What are the consequences of a principle like this? Well, it allows Wiccans to worship the creation, Mother Earth, rather than the Creator, God. New-Agers say that since we are all gods, we might as well get good at it. In Genesis 3:5 Satan deceitfully tells Adam and Eve that if they eat the fruit of a particular tree, they will be like God.

New Age teaching has reduced God to a human level so He's no different from you and me. If God is an impersonal force, He doesn't need to be served, obeyed, or loved. This is Satan's counterfeit for the one true God, the Father of our Lord Jesus Christ. Deuteronomy 6:4 NIV says, "The Lord our God, the Lord is one." In Ephesians 1:3 we read, "All praise to God, the Father of our Lord Jesus Christ."

God is not an "it" or a "force." He is our Father, the living and all-powerful God of creation. The Bible is filled with His attributes, and they tell us what kind of a great and awesome God He really is.

You are a little god. (self-realization)

New-Agers believe that since we are all gods, we must become "cosmically conscious" of the fact that we are gods. They say Jesus did that. He was nothing more than an enlightened master. He was a dynamic teacher and an incredible person because he came to grips with the fact that he was a little god. And just like Jesus, everyone else must come to realize that they, too, are gods, and start living like it.

New-Agers say, "We, too, share in the Christ-consciousness within us. The savior in us is replacing the Savior out there. There is no need for a Christ because we can save ourselves."

This principle is a counterfeit to what the Bible teaches. In Ephesians 2:8–9 we read, "God saved you by his grace when you believed. And you can't take credit for this; it is a gift from God. Salvation is not a reward for the good things we have done, so none of us can boast about it."

The Bible also says we are filled with hope as we wait for the glorious return of our great God and Savior, Jesus Christ (Titus 2:13). Jesus died on the cross to take the punishment for our sin. He paid our debt and died our death. Why? So we could experience new life and forgiveness for our sins. There is no second chance to come back and fix your mistakes. The Bible is very clear when it says we die only once and then we are judged (Hebrews 9:27).

Working toward a new world order.

New-Agers believe the countries of the world are coming together, and eventually national boundaries will no longer be necessary. People are all working to reach an "omega point"—ultimate peace. But it will happen only when we have a one-world government and a one-world religion.

Because of the unsettling world situation today, people are primed for someone to emerge as a leader, someone who will have the answers to all our problems. Someone who can lead the entire world. Many nations in Europe have already joined together to use one currency—the euro. Countries that were once divided are united again. New-Agers see all this as ushering in a new world order. This is a counterfeit of the kingdom of God.

The Bible teaches that only God will create a new heaven and earth (Isaiah 65:17). There will not be harmony or peace in this world until the Prince of Peace, Jesus, comes to live in the hearts of people.

Reality is what you make it.

New-Agers believe that reality is determined by what you believe. If you change what you believe, you can change reality. Because reality is what you make it, there is no such thing as moral absolutes or good and evil. Reality is what you think is good, even if someone else thinks it is evil.

A TV talk show host was interviewing the head of a very militant homosexual organization. This leader was pushing for the organization's members to start having sex with young children. The reporter was outraged and said so. The guest replied with, "Hey, lady, that is my truth. And even though it isn't your truth, it doesn't matter what you think."

What about premarital sex? The message from our society today is, "It's okay if you think it's okay. Just use a condom." Without moral absolutes, all sex is good sex, according to media therapists—as long as you think it's good.

The world is now a huge potpourri of "whatever." Everyone is developing his own ethics and codes of conduct, and the result is total confusion, total chaos.

The sense of good and evil has been placed in our hearts by God (Romans 2:15). Without any sense of right and wrong, this world is going to become a jungle. John 8:32 says that when you know the truth, it will set you free. Jesus said in John 14:6 NIV, "I am the way and the truth and the life. No one comes to the Father except through me." Absolute truth comes from God. Satan is saying it is all relative.

In some of your classrooms it's called "values clarification." You need to look to the Bible as your standard for right and wrong so you will know the difference.

A new way of thinking.

New-Agers believe we need to develop a new way of thinking about old problems. We need to think "holistically." If we are all interconnected particles in this cosmic ocean, and if we all are part of God, then we are able to think on one level. This new way of thinking comes only from a "mystical spiritual awakening" by getting in touch with your inner child.

But the Bible says we need to change the way we think by renewing our minds (Romans 12:2). By ourselves, we are capable of thinking only in human terms, but God can give us supernatural wisdom. Our new way of thinking also comes as a result of being new creations in Christ (2 Corinthians 5:17). The way to fully develop this new way of thinking is to allow God to readjust our minds, and this happens only through the study of His Word and by the power of the Holy Spirit.

New Age is a widespread and powerful phenomenon affecting our culture today. Its philosophy influences music, sports, literature—in fact, nothing seems exempt, not even some churches. In dealing with the New Age movement we are really dealing with spiritual warfare against the forces of darkness.

There are many dangers associated with New Age, but the biggest danger of all is that it keeps people who are searching for spiritual truth from finding the real thing—a personal relationship with Jesus Christ.

Watch for the trap of New Age thinking. Stay informed as to what is out there, and stay close to the Lord and in His Word. Be on the alert for subtle influences of New Age thinking trying to creep into your mind as Satan attempts to influence you.

WHAT IS THE OCCULT?

John Edward is a psychic medium, author, and lecturer who claims to have helped thousands over the last two decades with his supposed ability to predict future events and communicate with those who have crossed over to the "other side."

He's hosted a popular TV show, *Crossing Over*, on the Sci-Fi cable network. What most people don't realize is that John is using occult practices in his endeavors.

The word *occult* comes from the Latin word *occultus*, which means "hidden." But very little about the occult remains secret anymore. The activities, beliefs, practices, and rituals that have been traditionally considered of the occult are now well documented and published. Anyone can go to the library, a bookstore, or online to find information on just about any occult activity.

There are many definitions, and not a lot of agreement, on what is the occult. For the purposes of this chapter, let's use the following definition, which comes from the Ontario Consultants on Religious Tolerance.

> The occult is the most secret doctrine and mysterious practice involving the action or influence of supernatural agencies or some secret knowledge of them, which transcend the natural senses, to seek their influence in our present or future lives, or the lives of others.[4]

Because there's no real consensus on the exact meaning of what the occult is, there are some who would separate it into three main categories: divination, magick, and religious and spiritual pursuits.

Divination includes various techniques of predicting the future. These would include:

+ *Astrology*. The idea that your future is determined by the precise location of the sun, moon, and planets at the time of your birth.
+ *I Ching*. This is an ancient Chinese oracle book that some people believe can be used to answer questions and predict the future.

+ *Numerology*. The primary purpose of numerology is character analysis: to discover what "the above has to say to us below."
+ *Palm Reading*. Uses the creases in your palm and the shape of your fingers to predict your future.
+ *Runes*. Typically a group of sixteen to thirty-one letters (usually twenty-six) from an ancient Northern European alphabet. These letters are inscribed on pieces of plastic, paper, or small rocks. A group is tossed, and the future is predicted from the runes that land inverted and those face up, as well as from their position.
+ *Scrying*. A technique that involves gazing into a bowl of water, a black mirror, hot coals from a fire, or a crystal ball to produce visions of the future.
+ *Tarot Cards*. Fortune-telling through using a set of seventy-eight tarot cards. The cards are interpreted according to their inherent meaning, as modified by the importance of their position.
+ *Teacup Reading*. Shapes formed by tea leaves, after a cup of tea has been consumed, are used to predict the future.

Many other methods, including dice, dream interpretation, playing cards, pendulum movements, and dominos can also be used to foretell future events.

Magick involves practicing different kinds of rituals and spells as well as ceremonial magick. These are all used to change the environment and the material world to reach the objectives of the magician.

Religious and spiritual pursuits usually involve a collection of unrelated alternative religions, including syncretistic religions from the Caribbean like Vodun and Santeria, Satanism and Wicca, and Eastern religions like Hinduism, Buddhism, Taoism, etc.

Those involved in occult activities look at them as fascinating, harmless, mysterious, spiritual, and even a great source of healing power and knowledge. But there's another perspective that's important for us to look at: God's.

WHAT DOES THE BIBLE SAY ABOUT THE OCCULT?

The Bible leaves little doubt concerning how God feels about occult practices. Here are a few of the warnings in the Bible that talk about occult practices and reflect God's attitude toward them. Witchcraft, interpreting omens, telling the future based on signs, conjuring spells, and communicating with the dead are just a few of the occult things that are evil in the eyes of the Lord.

+ Leviticus 19:26—"Do not practice fortune-telling or witchcraft."
+ Leviticus 19:31—"Do not defile yourselves by turning to mediums or to those who consult the spirits of the dead. I am the Lord your God."
+ Leviticus 20:27—"Men and women among you who act as mediums or who consult the spirits of the dead must be put to death by stoning. They are guilty of a capital offense."
+ Deuteronomy 18:10–11—"Never sacrifice your son or daughter as a burnt offering. And do not let your people practice fortune-telling, or use sorcery, or interpret omens, or engage in witchcraft, or cast spells, or function as mediums or psychics, or call forth the spirits of the dead."
+ 2 Kings 21:6—"Manasseh also sacrificed his own son in the fire. He practiced sorcery and divination, and he

consulted with mediums and psychics. He did much that was evil in the Lord's sight, arousing his anger."

Even though you might be naturally curious about things like astrology, horoscopes, fortune-telling, witchcraft, and other practices, you have to remember that Satan is behind them. A lot of your interest and fascination with these things might come as a result of wanting to know and control the future. In the Bible, God tells us everything that we need to know about what is going to happen in the future.

The information that we receive through occult practices will be distorted and most of the time completely false because the source is bad—Satan and demons. But we can trust the guidance we receive through the Holy Spirit and the Bible. Since God created us, He knows what is best for us and will never lead us in the wrong direction or confuse us. But we must put all of our confidence in God and trust Him completely.

Check out this advice God gives us in Proverbs 3:5–6: "Trust in the Lord with all your heart; do not depend on your own understanding. Seek his will in all you do, and he will show you which path to take."

Don't try to figure out everything on your own. Listen for God's voice and watch for His direction everywhere you go and in everything you do.

But maybe you're still not convinced, because trusting in God seems so limiting and restrictive in an age of freedom and tolerance. Look at what the Bible says about occult practices in Isaiah 8:19: "Someone may say to you, 'Let's ask the mediums and those who consult the spirits of the dead. With their whisperings and mutterings, they will tell us what to do.' But shouldn't people ask God for guidance? Should the living seek guidance from the dead?"

Think logically for a minute: Why would you consult with witches and mediums who are trying to get answers from dead people? It makes much more sense to go to the living God for answers. Because God is eternal, He has already been to the future. Don't let anyone or anything take you away from the living and true God.

THINK ABOUT IT

1. Beside each of the six principles of New Age thinking listed below, write at least one place in our culture where you can see this kind of influence. Be specific.
   - All is one. One is all.
   - God is everything. Everything is God.
   - You are a little god.
   - Working toward a new world order.
   - Reality is what you make it.
   - A new way of thinking.
2. Read 1 Timothy 4:1–2. How do these verses relate to Satanism, New Age, and the occult? Be specific.
3. New-Agers are generally active in trying to address the problems in the world. As Christians, we should be even more active in making a difference. What one thing can you do this week to help deal with a problem or issue you see in your everyday life?
4. Why is it so hard to trust God for the future?

CHAPTER 9

VAMPIRES, GHOSTS, AND ANGELS

There's something about the supernatural that makes us curious. Whether it's vampires, ghosts, or angels, something inside of us wants to see how close we can get to them and find out if they're real. We see them in movies or on TV, and we start wondering: If vampires do exist, could they hurt me? Do they really drink blood? Or how about ghosts—how would I know if I actually saw one, and would it scare me? Are there really haunted houses? And when it comes to angels, the big question always seems to be: Do I really have a guardian angel? And if I do, can it protect me all the time, from everything?

In this chapter, we'll try to answer some of these questions and see what the Bible has to say about vampires, ghosts, and angels.

COUNT DRACULA AND THE BOYS IN THE 'HOOD

Vlad Tepes—Vlad the Impaler—was a fifteenth-century prince of Wallachia. He was also known as Dracula—the Dragon. Because of his murderous cruelty, he came to represent the type of vampire often associated with Halloween. According to the legend that started with Count Dracula, vampires are reanimated corpses that drink human blood and turn their victims into living corpses. Vampires supposedly take on the form of batlike demons.

It's a frightening truth that interest in vampires is popping up everywhere. This truth is revealed by how often they show up in movies, TV shows, books, role-playing games, Web sites, and even "vampire hunter" kits.

The classic book on vampires is Bram Stoker's gothic horror novel *Dracula*. Vampires are also a frequent topic in books by authors like Anne Rice. Then there's the long list of teen vampire books that includes *Companions of the Night* by Vivian Vande Velde and the VAMPIRE DIARIES series and *Soulmate Nightworld* by L. J. Smith.

Surf the Net and you'll find a lot of vampire Web sites. You can even take a survey online called "Am I a vampire?" There are chat rooms and support sites like "SphynxCat's Real Vampires Support Page." On *vampirehunters.com* you can buy a Vampire Hunter Kit. And if you really want to make a statement, you can order a bumper sticker that says, "Vampires suck!"

Today people can take a week-long Halloween trip to Transylvania, Romania—the fabled home of Count Dracula. The escorted tour explores the castles, graveyards, and legends of Romania. As part of the trip, guests can have the "ultimate experience" by spending Halloween night in Dracula's castle.

And think about Count Chocula breakfast cereal. Yes, there seems to be something for anyone who wants to dabble in the world of vampires.

ARE VAMPIRES REAL?

According to the Ancient Society of Vampire Hunters, there's a difference between true vampires and human ones. True vampires are supernatural undead creatures with specific identifying characteristics. These characteristics are lacking in the human vampires, who sometimes call themselves "real vampires," but are in reality simply misguided humans.

Real or fantasy, there are people who have bought in to this way of life and developed a morbid taste for blood. They're not like Hollywood's Dracula. These people have been deceived into believing that they've been changed and now possess immortality and supernatural powers, among other things, along with some specific weaknesses. They believe that they have an awesome capacity to absorb, channel, and manipulate "pranic energy," or life-force.

Becoming involved in these beliefs is really all about power and searching for it from a source other than God. The forces of darkness love to live out their deceptions in dumb humans who think it's fun to play around with stage blood and toy fangs.

WHAT DOES GOD THINK?

The word *vampire* is never mentioned in the Bible. But God does talk a lot about blood and power in His Word.

Blood is sacred to God, and the devil is perverting its meaning and importance, deceiving some people into thinking that by drinking blood, they can get power.

Here are just a few of the places God talks about blood:

+ "If any native Israelite or foreigner living among you eats or drinks blood in any form, I will turn against that person and cut him off from the community of your people, for the life of the body is in its blood. I have given you the blood on the altar to purify you, making you right with the Lord. It is the blood, given in exchange for a life, that makes purification possible. That is why I have said to the people of Israel, 'You must never eat or drink blood—neither you nor the foreigners living among you.'" Leviticus 17:10–12

+ "Never eat the blood, for the blood is the life, and you must not eat the lifeblood with the meat. Instead, pour out the blood on the ground like water. Do not eat the blood, so that all may go well with you and your children after you, because you will be doing what pleases the Lord." Deuteronomy 12:23–25

✦ "Anyone who eats my flesh and drinks my blood has eternal life, and I will raise that person at the last day. . . . Anyone who eats my flesh and drinks my blood remains in me, and I in him." John 6:54, 56

✦ "Without the shedding of blood, there is no forgiveness." Hebrews 9:22

✦ "For you know that God paid a ransom to save you from the empty life you inherited from your ancestors. And the ransom he paid was not mere gold or silver. It was the precious blood of Christ, the sinless, spotless Lamb of God." 1 Peter 1:18–19

There is no greater symbol of life than blood because without blood, we are physically dead. This is true spiritually as well. Without the blood of a perfect sacrifice to pay for our sins, God says we are spiritually dead and will be eternally separated from Him. In the Old Testament, the shed blood from animal sacrifices temporarily brought forgiveness for those who confessed their sins. In the New Testament Jesus became the ultimate, perfect, permanent sacrifice when He shed His blood for our sins. He was the perfect sacrifice because He never sinned. From the time of Christ's sacrificial death on the cross, there is forgiveness and spiritual life only through that sacrificial blood. When we accept this shed blood for our sins in faith, then we will receive life—meaningful and eternal. Peter reminds us that the blood of Christ is precious (1 Peter 1:19). And anyone who understands what Christ did on the cross would agree.

Those who take on the sacrifice of Christ's blood for the

forgiveness of their sins are called "Christians" or "Christ followers." In memory of Christ's death, Christians take Communion—a piece of bread as symbolic of Christ's body, and a little
wine or juice as symbolic of His blood sacrifice. In John 6, Jesus
is not saying to "eat Him" literally but that He is going to give
His life for us.

That's why Jesus is the source of life and gives us the real
power we need to deal with the challenges and issues of life. We
have no power apart from God's Spirit. God demonstrated His
mighty power when He brought Jesus back to life from the grave
and when He took Him back up into heaven after the resurrection. Think about the power that it takes to launch the space
shuttle off the pad and out into space. Or the power it takes to
send an unmanned mission to Mars. It's incredible physical
power. But God gives us unbelievable spiritual power. And here's
the awesome thing—we don't have to go bite someone on the
neck or drink blood. Christians already have this power; we just
need to recognize that we have it and use it! (Ephesians 1:19–20;
Acts 1:8; 2 Timothy 1:7)

DO GHOSTS EXIST?

Growing up in northern California, I spent a lot of time camp-
ing with my family and friends. Whether we were at the beach
or in the mountains, at night we would all sit around the fire,
eating s'mores and listening to someone tell ghost stories. Sometimes on Saturday morning TV we would watch scary movies
about ghosts or see *Casper the Friendly Ghost* cartoons. And each
time we made a trip down to Disneyland, we'd go on the
Haunted Mansion ride. Besides seeing spirits popping out from
various parts of the old mansion, we also saw ghosts that
appeared to be dancing in the ballroom and ones that would

mysteriously appear next to us in the car that takes you through the second half of the ride. These hitchhikers made us scream or laugh—depending on how old we were at the time.

It seems that there is a lot of talk about ghosts today. Ghosts seem to be popping up everywhere from movies like *Pirates of the Caribbean* and *Ghostrider* to TV shows like *Ghost Whisperer*. There are people who claim to have seen ghosts and even captured them on film. Forty-two percent of Americans believe that houses can be haunted, and 38 percent believe that ghosts or spirits of dead people can come back in certain places and situations.[1] People even take castle-hopping trips in search of ghosts and spirits in England, Scotland, and Ireland.

But do ghosts really exist? The Bible is pretty clear about saying that the spirit world is swarming with life. God himself is a Spirit (John 4:24), and of course there's the Holy Spirit of God (called the "Holy Ghost" in some Bible translations). The Bible also says that God created countless angels, most of whom are "good." We also learn from God's Word that one-third of the angels rebelled and sinned against God. These fallen angels are called demons, of which Satan himself is one. But what are ghosts? Are they spirits of people who have died?

There's only one place where the Bible talks about the spirit of a dead person appearing to someone—when Samuel appeared to Saul in the Old Testament. (Saul consulted a medium, something God forbids.) As we look at this story, it's important to remember that if this was actually the spirit of Samuel, this was an unusual occasion to deliver an important message, not one to scare or haunt someone.

> "Don't be afraid!" the king told her. "What do you see?"
> "I see a god coming up out of the earth," she said.
> "What does he look like?" Saul asked.

"He is an old man wrapped in a robe," she replied.

Saul realized it was Samuel, and he fell to the ground before him. "Why have you disturbed me by calling me back?" Samuel asked Saul.

"Because I am in deep trouble," Saul replied. "The Philistines are at war with me, and God has left me and won't reply by prophets or dreams. So I have called for you to tell me what to do."

But Samuel replied, "Why ask me, since the Lord has left you and has become your enemy? The Lord has done just as he said he would. He has torn the kingdom from you and given it to your rival, David. The Lord has done this to you today because you refused to carry out his fierce anger against the Amalekites. What's more, the Lord will hand you and the army of Israel over to the Philistines tomorrow, and you and your sons will be here with me. The Lord will bring down the entire army of Israel in defeat."

Saul fell full length on the ground, paralyzed with fright because of Samuel's words. He was also faint with hunger, for he had eaten nothing all day and all night. (1 Samuel 28:13–20)

There are two places in the New Testament that mention ghosts, but both times it was a misperception on the part of the disciples. Here's one example from Matthew; the other one is found in Luke 24.

About three o'clock in the morning Jesus came toward them, walking on the water. When the disciples saw him walking on the water, they were terrified. In their fear, they cried out, "It's a ghost!" But Jesus spoke to them at once. "Don't be afraid," he said. "Take courage. I am here!" (Matthew 14:25–27)

Throughout biblical history angels appear to people, but never in a haunting way. Usually they appear in some "human form" and clearly identify themselves and their message or mission from God.

So do ghosts really exist? If they aren't angels or spirits of dead people, the only other reasonable possibility is that ghosts are probably demons. If this is true, then there's nothing we have to be afraid of—if we have put our faith and trust in Jesus. But ghosts—whether demons or some other spirit being—are something that we should steer clear of, as 1 Thessalonians 5:22 reminds us to do when it says, "Stay away from every kind of evil."

TOUCHED BY AN ANGEL

I think we'd be remiss if we didn't discuss angels here as well. There was a time when you encountered angels mostly in manger scenes and as Christmas ornaments. And don't forget some of the golden oldie songs like "Earth Angel" and "You Are My Special Angel," and the more contemporary hit by The Newsboys, "Entertaining Angels."

When angel mania flooded popular culture, angels were everywhere, from little ceramic figurines to prime-time TV shows like the former surprise hit *Touched by an Angel*. Angels-only boutiques appeared along with angel newsletters and seminars. Revered universities have courses on angels. There are even workshops available to teach you how to unleash your "inner angel." So why the big interest in angels?

A book called *Angels Among Us*, by Ron Rhodes, lists some of the reasons today's "angel experts" suggest for the rise in angel popularity:

+ Angels supposedly offer humankind a form of spirituality that does not involve commitment to God or the laws of God.

+ Angels are thought to be a means of attaining God's help without having to deal directly with God.

+ Angels have allegedly stepped up their activity among human beings in recent years in order to help them.

+ Guardian angels are popular today because of people's perceived need for protection in an often-threatening world.

+ Angel worship is a reaction against the materialism and secularism of Western society.

+ Angels are believed to bring meaning and purpose into our lives.

+ Angels allegedly give assurance to people regarding life after death.[2]

Did you notice that most of the excitement people have today about angels is based in recklessly unbiblical ideas? In fact, a lot of what's being taught today about angels has more to do with fallen angels (demons) than God's holy angels.

The Bible is the best source to learn all about angels. God is the creator of angels (Colossians 1:16), and He's the one who can tell us the real facts we need to know about them.

ARE ANGELS REAL?

Dr. S. W. Mitchell, a Philadelphia neurologist, had gone to bed after a really long day. Suddenly someone knocking on his door awakened him. Opening it, he found a little girl, poorly dressed and very upset. She told him her mother was very sick and asked if he would please come with her. It was a bitterly cold, snowy night, and even though he was bone tired, Dr. Mitchell dressed and followed the girl.

He found the mother desperately ill with pneumonia. After arranging for medical care, he complimented the sick woman on the intelligence and persistence of her little daughter. The woman looked at him strangely and said, "My daughter died a month ago." She added, "Her shoes and coat are in the clothes closet there." Mitchell, amazed and perplexed, went to the closet and opened the door. There hung the very coat worn by the little girl who had brought him to tend to her mother. It was warm and dry and could not possibly have been worn in the wintry night.[3]

Could the doctor have been called in the hour of desperate need by an angel who appeared as this woman's daughter? Was this the work of God's angels on behalf of the sick woman?

John G. Paton was a missionary in the New Hebrides Islands. Hostile natives surrounded his mission headquarters one night, intent on burning the Patons out and killing them. John and his wife prayed all during that terror-filled night that God would rescue them. When daylight came, they were amazed to see the attackers leave. They thanked God for rescuing them.

A year later, the chief of the tribe accepted Christ, and Mr. Paton, remembering what had happened, asked the chief what had kept him and his men from burning down the house and killing him and his wife. The chief replied in surprise, "Who were all those men you had with you there?" The missionary told him there had been no men there, only him and his wife. The chief argued that they had seen many men standing guard— hundreds of big men in shining garments with drawn swords in their hands. They seemed to circle the mission station so that the natives were afraid to attack. Only then did Mr. Paton realize that God had sent His angels to protect them. The chief agreed that there was no other explanation.[4] Could it be that God had sent a legion of angels to protect Paton and his wife, whose lives were endangered?

The Bible clearly teaches there can be no question that

angels do exist. There are more than one hundred references to angels in the Old Testament, while the New Testament mentions them about 165 times. Their existence is mentioned in thirty-four books of the Bible (seventeen in the Old Testament and seventeen in the New Testament), from Job to Revelation. Even Jesus referred to angels as real beings.

Angels are ambassadors of God. They're part of His heavenly court and service. Angels are created beings according to Psalm 148:5. They did not evolve from some lower or less-complicated form of life. They cannot procreate, for Matthew 22:30 tells us that at the resurrection, people will be like angels, neither marrying nor being given in marriage. The Bible does not specifically state the time of their creation, but since they were present when the earth was created (Job 38:7), their creation had to be before earth's.

Originally, all angelic creatures were created holy, but Revelation 12:4 tells us that when sin entered the world through Adam and Eve, one-third of all the angels joined Satan, rebelled against God, and became demons. God's good angels—the ones who did not rebel against Him—are called holy in Mark 8:38.

Angels are different from human beings. As creatures they are limited in knowledge, power, and activity (1 Peter 1:11–12; Revelation 7:1), and like all responsible creatures, they will be subject to judgment (Matthew 25:41; 1 Corinthians 6:3).

WHAT ARE ANGELS LIKE?

In Hebrews 1:14 NIV, angels are called "ministering spirits," suggesting that they don't have physical bodies. Consequently, they don't function as human beings and aren't subject to death as we are. They also don't have the same limitations as people. Angels have greater power and wisdom than we do, although God still limits these.

Angels are limited, compared to us, in other ways. Since they're not created in the image of God, they cannot share in our final destiny with Jesus. The Bible teaches that eventually followers of Jesus will be lifted above the angels (1 Corinthians 6:3).

Usually angels emerge as men and have appeared in dreams and visions (Matthew 1:20; Isaiah 6:1–8), in special signs of their presence (2 Kings 6:17), and to people in a normal, conscious, waking state (Genesis 19:1–8; Mark 16:5). Some angels do have wings (Isaiah 6:2, 6), and in some heavenly visions they possess superhuman characteristics.

The number of angels is so huge they can't even be counted (Revelation 5:11), and there's a vast organization and ranking of angels. The Bible speaks of the "assembly" and the "council" of angels (Psalm 89:5, 7 NIV), of their organization for battle (Revelation 12:7), and even of various ranks of archangels, chief princes, governmental rulers, cherubim, and seraphim.

Without a doubt, God has organized the good angels, and Satan has organized the evil ones. Only Michael is designated as the archangel, or high-ranking angel (Jude 9:l; 1 Thessalonians 4:16). He leads the angelic armies of heaven against Satan and forces of evil, and in the book of Daniel he appears as the guardian angel of Israel, who will be of special help during her time of trouble.

Other prominent individual angels are mentioned in the Bible, including Gabriel. Gabriel's name means "hero of God," and he appears to be a high-ranking angel. His function has been to bring important messages from God to several people. Gabriel is important to the Christmas story, because he's the one who told Mary she would bear the son of God and that her baby would be great and would rule on the throne of David (Luke 1:26–27). Lucifer (Satan) was an anointed cherub. He fell from his original high position and led a host of angels in his rebellion against God (Ezekiel 28:16–17; Revelation 12:4).

WHAT DO ANGELS DO?

Good angels are basically servants. Hebrews 1:14 says, "Angels are only servants—spirits sent to care for people who will inherit salvation." Besides their ministry to believers, angels also have a ministry to God, and they even have a relationship to non-Christians.

Their primary ministry to God is to worship and praise Him. The cherubim defend His holiness, while the seraphim surround His throne and attend to His holiness. The Bible also tells us angels praise Him (Isaiah 6:3), worship Him (Revelation 5:8–13), rejoice in what He does (Job 38:6–7), serve Him (Psalm 103:20), and act as instruments of His judgment (Revelation 7:1, 8:2). Angels also seem to be very active when God starts a new era in history. For example, angels joined in praise when the earth was created (Job 38:6–7), they were involved in the giving of the Mosaic Law (Galatians 3:19; Hebrews 2:2), and they were active during the beginning years of the early Church (Acts 8:26; 10:3–7; 12:11).

Plus, angels have an important ministry to Jesus, from before His birth until His Second Coming. Just as angelic beings surround the throne of the Father, so the angels also attend to God the Son. An angel announced the birth of Christ to the shepherds and was then accompanied in praise by a multitude of other angels (Luke 2:8–15), and angels protected Jesus when he was a baby. It was an angel that warned Joseph and Mary to flee to Egypt to escape Herod's wrath (Matthew 2:13–15) and an angel that instructed the couple when it was safe to return to the land of Israel (Matthew 2:19–20).

Angels encouraged Jesus after the forty days of temptation (Matthew 4:1–11) and strengthened Him in difficult times in the garden of Gethsemane (Luke 22:43). The Lord himself said that legions of angels stood ready to come to His defense if called upon (Matthew 26:53).

It was an angel that rolled away the stone from Christ's tomb (Matthew 28:1–2), announced His resurrection to the women on that first Easter morning (Luke 24:5–7), and reminded the women of Jesus' earlier promise to rise on the third day. Angels also were present when Jesus was taken back up to heaven (Acts 1:10–11), and will prepare the world for and participate in the second coming of Jesus Christ.

Angels have a unique relationship to those who do not have a relationship with God, because they will be involved in carrying out judgment. They will announce impending judgments to unbelievers (Genesis 19:13; Revelation 14:6–7), inflict those judgments on the unrighteous (Acts 12:23), and will separate the righteous from the unrighteous (Matthew 13:39–40).

God's angels have also been commissioned and sent out with the responsibility of aiding believers. They minister to us personally, offering encouragement, protection, and provision at the Lord's request. When Paul was caught in a storm at sea, an angel encouraged him, reminding Paul that he would arrive safely in Rome to be a witness for Christ (Acts 27:23–25). It was an angel that protected David when he was forced to flee the Philistines (Psalm 34:7), and an angel offered Elijah nourishment when he was weak in the middle of a lengthy journey (1 Kings 19:5–7).

Philip received direction from an angel to witness to the Ethiopian official (Acts 8:26), and an angel arranged the meeting of Cornelius and Peter that resulted in a lot of people accepting Christ (Acts 10:3–22). There also seems to be a connection between the prayer for Peter's release from prison and the angel's releasing him (Acts 12:1–11), and in a similar way, Daniel's prayer was explained by an angel (Daniel 9:20–27).

Angels aid in bringing people to Jesus (Acts 8:26; 10:3) and care for Christians at the time of death. Luke 16:22 describes the death of Lazarus and the angels carrying him to Abraham's side.

Without question the most popular and controversial aspect of angels has to do with their role as the guardians of God's people. The idea of individual guardian angels is popular today among New Age angel enthusiasts, and there are even some Bible scholars who say that every single believer has a personal guardian angel that stays with him or her throughout life.

There are two main places in the Bible that relate to the idea of guardian angels. Matthew 18:10 reads, "Beware that you don't look down on any of these little ones. For I tell you that in heaven their angels are always in the presence of my heavenly Father." The second place is found in Acts 12:15. In this incident we find a servant girl named Rhoda recognizing Peter's voice outside the door of the house while the people inside, thinking Peter was still in jail, said, "You're out of your mind." When she kept insisting it was true, they said, "It must be his angel." Some Bible scholars have concluded from these two verses that every Christian must have a guardian angel. One thing's for sure: Whether we have one angel or a bunch of them watching over us, we need to become more aware of the fact that God does provide angelic protection for us. No matter how many angels are involved, we should be a lot less fearful of our circumstances and our enemies. Imagine how different our lives would be if we could recognize God's constant provision of angels to protect us.

Angels are closer than we think. There are millions of angels who are at God's command to help you and me with the issues of life at home, at school, and everywhere else. Be encouraged that God has ordered "his angels to protect you wherever you go. They will hold you up with their hands so you won't even hurt your foot on a stone" (Psalm 91:11–12).

One final warning, though. Even though angels are God's messengers, false angels (probably fallen angels—demons) can try to mislead you. If the angel is truly from God, he will not steer you wrong. Remember what the Bible says: "Let God's curse fall on anyone, including us or even an angel from heaven, who preaches a different kind of Good News than the one we preached to you" (Galatians 1:8).

Think about it

1. Do stories about vampires and ghosts encourage us to be interested in the occult? Why would this be bad for a Christian?

2. Read Jude 8–10. How does God want us to respond to supernatural spiritual beings?

3. If someone is having trouble dealing with certain kinds of fear, how could it help to understand what God's angels do?

4. How can you practically avoid different forms of evil? Be specific.

PART THREE

STANDING UP
TO THE DEVIL

CHAPTER 10

TAKE CONTROL

I met Robert at a high school summer camp that I was speaking at in central California. He was into music—thrash, metal, and alternative—so because of my background as a drummer we hit it off right away. In conversations I sensed something was really bothering Robert, but I couldn't figure out what it was.

On Thursday night, at the end of one of my talks, I gave everyone the opportunity to put his or her faith and trust in Jesus. Robert was one of the first to stand up and indicate he had made this commitment. After the meeting was over, Robert's youth pastor asked if I could talk to him for a few minutes.

Robert opened up to me about how rough his life had been. He had been worshiping Satan after a friend convinced him his life would be better if he did. Robert explained how he and his friend got into all kinds of evil stuff. They smoked marijuana and crystal meth. Together they studied the *Satanic Bible* and asked the Ouija board for answers about life.

When he got to camp, every time I spoke, Robert said he would hear a strange voice in his head say, "I love you and want to make your life better. Don't listen to Steve." But Robert kept listening anyway—to every one of my messages. He gradually began to sense that something was missing in his life.

By Thursday night, Robert realized that it was Jesus who was missing from his life. At that point the voice in his head got violent and said, "If you turn to Christ, I'm going to kill you." Robert made the decision anyway, knowing it was the right thing to do. But he was frightened about what might happen next.

I reassured Robert that he'd done the right thing and that he could trust God to protect him. One of the first verses I shared with him was 1 John 4:4: "You belong to God, my dear children. You have already won a victory over those people, because the Spirit who lives in you is greater than the spirit who lives in the world."

Robert realized that he'd been living a lie for several years. He knew there'd be a lot of changes happening in his life now that he belonged to Jesus. Not too long ago, I spoke with one of the staff members at Robert's church and found out that he was still hanging in there on the commitment he had made at camp. It hadn't been easy, but it had definitely been worth it. Robert took a bold stand against the devil and won. And so can you.

You're not alone in the spiritual battle. God is ready, willing, and able to help you. In these final chapters, we'll be looking at how to defend ourselves against Satan's attacks. And we'll start with learning how to take control of our mind.

PREPARE YOUR MIND FOR BATTLE

Years ago, radio host and author Paul Harvey told the story of how naval academy graduates in Japan, beginning in 1931, were asked the question: "How would you carry out a surprise attack on Pearl Harbor?" In February of 1932, the Japanese received an answer that they believed was a foolproof plan, but the question remained on each exam for the next nine years.

In the fall of 1941, a Japanese ship arrived at Honolulu with four naval experts assigned to test the plan they had hatched in 1932. Disguised as stewards, these officers took plenty of shore leave, saw the sights, took photos, and even took tourist plane rides over Pearl Harbor—plus more photos. The consulate gave these Japanese "stewards" maps of Pearl Harbor and the military airfields. They even purchased souvenir sets of postcards containing aerial shots of Battleship Row and the docking area by Ford Island.

One month later a fleet of Japanese naval ships arrived in Hawaii, only this time it was for an attack. On December 7, 1941, Japan took the United States military completely by surprise. In 110 minutes, 8 large battleships and 3 light cruisers were sunk or damaged, 188 planes were destroyed, and 2,400 men were killed.

The attack not only paralyzed the U.S. military in the Pacific for almost a year, but it also exposed the unbelievable fact that we were not ready for battle.[1] Our military had been taken completely off guard with this surprise attack. An investigation later showed that soldiers manning a radar station early on the morning of December 7 had actually seen the Japanese planes approaching Pearl Harbor. But because they were unprepared for a possible attack, these soldiers thought what they were seeing on the radar screen was American planes, and they failed to verify this with anyone else. By the time they realized what was really happening, it was too late. Had Pearl Harbor been on the alert and prepared for action, who knows how many lives could have been saved on December 7.

The damage Satan can cause in your life may not be in terms of casualties and equipment loss, but he can make you miserable, angry, and bitter, and sidetrack you from God's path for your life. Are you prepared for action so this doesn't happen? Are you on the alert for a possible attack? Remember, ultimately, it's a battle for the mind that must be won.

Here are some ideas to help you take control of your thoughts and win the battle for your mind.

Be on the alert

My good friend Bill was a fireman in Seattle. One late night I was on the phone with him while he was at the fire station. In the middle of our conversation, the alarm at the station house went off. Bill said, "Sorry, Steve. That sound means I gotta go. Talk with you later." And he was gone! During every shift that Bill worked at the fire station, he had to be alert and prepared for emergency action at any time—even in the middle of the night.

Are you prepared in the same way when it comes to the battle for your mind? First Peter 1:13 tells us to prepare our minds for action and be self-controlled. In other words, get serious about the spiritual battle for your mind. Put your mind on alert for anything and everything that may distract you from clear and obedient thinking. Don't just sit around and see what happens. There's important work to be accomplished to protect your mind.

You must be careful what you expose your mind to at all times. Don't forget Satan is sneaky and masquerades as an angel of light (2 Corinthians 11:14). He will attack you from any direction and at any time. Being prepared means that you are not only ready for action but that you have the proper and necessary equipment for battle as well. (We'll talk more about this later in chapters 13 and 14: "Combat Ready" and "Choose Your Weapons.")

If you are prepared for action and on the alert, you will be able to protect your mind—and what goes in it—from the attacks of the Enemy.

Guard your mind

While on a ministry trip to the Philippines, we stayed at a large multistoried hotel. When we checked in, I noticed armed guards everywhere. Twenty-four hours a day these guards stood at the front doors of the hotel, checking everyone who tried to enter. There were also guards on every floor of the hotel protecting the rooms. Each time we got off the elevator to head to our rooms, the guards would ask for our name and room number, and then they would write something in a record book. They were being extremely careful not to let anyone in the hotel or in a room who didn't belong there.

The same principle should apply to our minds. Proverbs 4:23 says, "Guard your heart above all else, for it determines the course of your life." As I mentioned in an earlier chapter, this use of the word *heart* refers to the mind as the center for thinking and reason. But it also includes the emotions, the will—basically our whole inner being: our purposes, intentions, understanding, and knowledge.

Because the devil assaults us from many directions with every conceivable form of evil, our minds must be strongly guarded. We must become aware of our weak points mentally—where we are vulnerable to Satan's evil enticements and his influence over our thinking.

The objective is to not allow evil in any form into our minds. We don't want to give the devil any kind of foothold in our thinking process (Ephesians 4:27). Our minds are constantly gathering and storing information, just like a digital camera or an mp3. We need to stop consuming anything and everything available to us for entertainment and amusement without recognizing that not all of it is good for our mental and spiritual life.

It's not easy to erase the DVDs of our mind. I'm not proud of some of the things that I put into my mind before I was a Christian. And it's amazing to me how Satan loves to do instant replays in my mind of some of these things. Closely guard what gets "recorded" because it may continue to influence your thinking long after you first saw or heard it.

It's been said that if the fortress is taken, the entire town must surrender. If the Enemy captures the mind, the whole person—affections, desires, motives, and actions—is hostage. Ultimately, to guard our minds means we must safeguard our eyes and ears, because they are the potential entry points for evil. Protecting our minds from what goes in is the first step toward changing our thinking and our actions.

Change the way you think

My car was running lousy, so I took it to the shop. The mechanic found a couple of problems, but he said the main culprit was the type of gas I was using—the octane level wasn't high enough. After getting the repairs and buying different gasoline, the car ran fine.

Sometimes our lives are not running smoothly because we are putting the wrong "fuel" into our minds. We need to change the input so we can change the way we think and ultimately the way we live. But we can't do this alone. We need God's help.

The apostle Paul writes in Romans 12:2, "Don't copy the behavior and customs of this world, but let God transform you into a new person by changing the way you think." Because Satan is the god of this world, he shapes contemporary thinking and values, which then form the moral climate of society. God wants us to stop buying in to this way of thinking and living. But this can only happen when we change the way we think.

God wants to change what's going on in the "control center" of our attitudes, thoughts, feelings, and actions. This is accomplished when we saturate ourselves in God's Word. The Holy Spirit then takes what we have read, studied, and memorized from the Bible to change our thinking. This needs to be a regular part of our life if we want to grow spiritually and have victory in the battle for our mind. I have a friend named Charlie who is in his eighties and is one of my spiritual heroes. He has a simple motto: "No Bible, no breakfast." He's not being legalistic and hard-nosed. Charlie is just saying we should make spiritual nourishment a priority in our life. Few of us would miss eating a meal, yet we find it so easy to skip a "spiritual meal"—sometimes for days or weeks at a time. It comes down to choosing what is right, not what is convenient.

Have you made an adjustment in the things you put into your mind? Colossians 3:1–2 gives us this advice: "Since you have been raised to new life with Christ, set your sights on the realities of heaven, where Christ sits in the place of honor at God's right hand. Think about the things of heaven, not the things of earth." Just like a compass points north, so should the attitude of our mind point us toward heaven and the things that please God. Our "heavenly thoughts" should be a filter, a lens through which we look at life.

Take control

If we are going to be successful at staying alert, guarding our minds, and changing the way we think, we have to take control of our thoughts. God gives us some advice for accomplishing this in 2 Corinthians 10:3–5:

> We are human, but we don't wage war as humans do. We use God's mighty weapons, not worldly weapons, to knock down the strongholds of human reasoning and to destroy false arguments. We destroy every proud obstacle that keeps people from knowing God. We capture their rebellious thoughts and teach them to obey Christ.

God wants us to run every thought through a "spiritual filtering system" to find the ones that contradict His truth, and then destroy their influence in our lives by not allowing them into our minds.

The best filtering system is not Christian music or even what other Christians say—it's the Bible. God's Word is filled with many verses we can use to filter our thoughts so they become pleasing to God. It's worth repeating: Philippians 4:8 is one of the best verses to apply as a filter for our thinking—whether it's music, movies, games, or something we are reading.

When we use a biblical filter, we compare what goes into our mind with God's Word to see if it is something we should think about. If it isn't, we should immediately tune it out or turn it off. By using the Bible, we are not dealing with someone else's opinion or even taste, but with the source of all truth. And when we fill our minds with the teaching of God's truth, we live the truth rather than the devil's lies.

But why should you have to filter every thought? Maybe this will help. When I was in South America I had the chance to go to a snake farm. It was weird to stand alongside a huge pit, filled with all kinds of poisonous snakes. I'm not a big fan of snakes—especially looking down on hundreds of them, making the ground appear as if it were moving—but it was a fascinating place to visit. Venom from the snakes was used to make antidotes to give to people who got bit. This particular facility shipped antidote serum to a lot of places in the world. One of the staff members said that with some poisonous snakes, all it takes is a few drops of their venom to kill you. In the same way, Satan doesn't need a whole lot of poisonous ideas to get a foothold in our lives through our minds.

Have you ever wondered why you struggle with bad attitudes toward your parents, a friend, or a teacher, or why you have to take eighteen cold showers before you go on a date to control your passion, or why you do some of the crazy things you do? It all has to do with what you've been putting in your mind—what you read, watch, and listen to.

The most effective way to use this "filtering system" is to keep it with you all the time. While we can't always carry a Bible around with us every place we go, we can memorize verses that apply to the mind—like Proverbs 4:23 or Philippians 4:8—so that the filter is always in place and ready to use. Check out Psalm 119:9–11:

> How can a young person stay pure? By obeying your word. I have tried hard to find you—don't let me wander from your commands. I have hidden your word in my heart, that I might not sin against you.

By hiding God's Word in your heart—memorizing it—your mind is always on the alert. When some bit of satanic "wisdom" or empty philosophy makes an attempt to creep into your thoughts, the filtering system is there to help you keep out evil and harmful things.

And I can tell you from personal experience that it really does work!

My ministry team and I were in Stockholm, Sweden, for a day and a half on our way home from an evangelistic campaign in Riga, Latvia—one of the Baltic republics. A couple of guys from the team and I decided to go to a movie. After a brief search we discovered a theater that was showing two films in English—a British version of *Robin Hood* and also *Predator 2*. We were in the mood for an action film, and one of the guys thought Arnold Schwarzenegger was starring in *Predator 2*, so we bought the tickets and went inside.

We quickly realized that we'd confused *Terminator 2* with

Predator 2. There was more sex, occult violence, and gore in the first fifteen minutes of the movie than I'd seen in a long, long time. As I watched, I kept wondering if the film was ever going to get better. But it didn't. Finally my spiritual filtering system clicked in, and a little voice inside my mind said, *Hey, Russo. This stuff isn't true, good, and right. So stop letting it into your mind and get outta here!*

My next thought was, *What will my friends think?* I quickly realized it didn't matter what they thought. I knew what I had to do to protect my mind. I told the other guys that I couldn't watch this stuff anymore, and I walked out. After I explained to the manager why I left, he said I could get my money back or go see *Robin Hood* instead. Within a few minutes my friends had also left *Predator 2* and joined me to watch a pretty dry and boring version of *Robin Hood.* Filtering worked for me, and it can work for you.

It's okay to filter. There's nothing wrong with leaving a movie that's bad or logging off a Web site that's raunchy or stopping the DVD player if the movie you've rented isn't really something you should be watching. And you can even exercise the muscle in your index finger to change the frequency on the FM dial to listen to a more positive tune. Society (including some of your friends!) may think it's strange, but following God's advice about this dimension of your life is the best thing you could do. And who knows, just maybe some of your friends will catch on and see the benefits of "taking control."

Filtering isn't always easy, but it's always worth it. You may take some heat from family or friends, but God will honor your decision. He may also use you to set an example for others about how important it is to guard your mind. When you find yourself in a position with a group of people and you feel the need to stop watching or listening to something, don't make a big scene.

Just quietly do whatever needs to be done (walk out, leave the room, etc.). If someone asks why you left, in a nonjudgmental way explain that what everyone is watching or listening to isn't right for you, and that you've made a choice to be more selective in your entertainment. If you take a positive approach to sharing your convictions, it may open the door for you to explain more of the "why" with your friends, including a chance to tell them about Jesus.

TAKE THE "RUSSO CHALLENGE"

Here's an experiment to consider. I call it the Russo Challenge. For one week don't turn on your mp3 player, watch TV, go to a movie, play a computer game, or surf the Net for entertainment purposes. In other words, turn it all off—even if it's Christian. Some might call this an entertainment fast. Use the time you normally would spend on entertainment to spend time in God's Word. Take time to meditate on (think deeply about) what you're learning from the Bible, and ask God how it applies to your life. Turn to Him in prayer for answers to questions in your life. Give the Lord a chance to really clean out your mind and change your thinking—without any distractions.

You'll be amazed at what will happen. Your attitudes about certain things, people, and situations in your life will improve. You'll notice a new sense of self-control and peace. And you will take on a more hopeful perspective about any problems in life. All of this and more will take place because you will be much more aware of God's perspective rather than the world's.

During week two of the Russo Challenge, don't turn on your mp3 player, switch on the satellite dish, or surf the Net until you've been in God's Word and spent time in prayer. To help remind you, take several three-by-five index cards and print in big, bold letters BOOK on each one. Place them in your room, locker, on the front of your skateboard, in your car—anywhere you will see them frequently each day. And don't even think about using some lame excuse like, "I just don't have enough time 'cause I'm so busy with everything else in my life." That's not a very valid reason. No matter how busy we get, we can always find time to do what we want to do. Ask God to change your attitude and your priorities.

If you're not sure where to start reading, here are a couple of ideas. Start with the book of Proverbs. There's one chapter of Proverbs for every day of the month, so you'll never forget where you are supposed to be. Then pick one verse from each chapter to memorize. It's a great place to get godly wisdom for everyday living. Or begin with one of the gospels: Matthew, Mark, Luke, or John. Read a chapter a day. My personal favorite is the book of Mark because it reads almost like a newspaper, and we see Jesus interacting with a lot of different people in different situations. Each week find a verse that really hits home for you and memorize it. Write it out on a three-by-five card or text it in your cell phone so you can carry it around with you and review it several times a day. And don't forget to spend time each day in prayer talking with God.

After you complete the second week, just continue doing the same thing each day. There's no telling how dramatically your life may change if you get serious about taking control of your mind!

Finally, here are a couple more things to think about with the Russo Challenge. First, why not propose the challenge to family members and friends? Your example may be all they need. Second, send me an email if you take the challenge. Let me know how it worked for you and if you've noticed any changes in your attitudes. I want to encourage you in the stand you've taken. You'll find my contact information in the back of the book.

Nothing is more important than taking control of your mind. That's where the battle is not only waged but where it will be won or lost! Reread this chapter if necessary, and put the things we've discussed into practice. God is more than willing to help us, but we must have the desire to change and make an effort to be obedient to the truth of His Word. Nothing has greater potential to change our lives than winning the battle for our mind.

Get serious and take control!

Think about it

1. Read Isaiah 26:3 and Philippians 4:7. What are some of the positive benefits when you keep your mind focused on God?
2. What does it mean to renew your mind (Romans 12:2)? What areas of your thought life need to be changed? Be specific.
3. Read Matthew 22:37. What steps are you taking to fulfill the commandment of loving God with all your mind? What would have to change for you to accomplish this?

CHAPTER 11

OUR DEFENDER

Shortly after talking about kids and Satanism on the national radio program *Focus on the Family,* I received a call from a high school counselor. She was deeply concerned about the number of students on her campus who were dabbling in Satanism and the occult. More than 150 teens had been referred for professional counseling in the first six weeks of school because of their involvement. "You must do something to help us," she pleaded. "The problem is getting worse."

"Could you give me a profile of the typical student who is involved?" I asked. Without hesitation she responded, "They're all churched kids. I think they've been given a taste of the supernatural but have never been given the real thing."

These days, there's unending interest and hunger for what's real. Just look at the popularity of reality TV shows, where we see inside someone's day-to-day life. That's why it seems crazy that when you start discussing the reality of Jesus, people get skeptical. Why is it so difficult to believe that we can actually *know* the Son of God? It's because that's part of the spiritual battle—part of Satan's plan. The devil wants us to doubt that Jesus is more than just a good teacher so that we'll continue to reject Him as our Savior and Lord. But if we do put our faith and trust in Jesus, Satan wants us to doubt that we can depend on Him to be our defender—the one who ultimately protects us in the heat of spiritual warfare.

Do you know the real Jesus? I'm talking about the Jesus of the Bible, not the Jesus whose name is thrown around the locker room or mocked in some movie or song. Let's look at a couple of examples of how mixed up some people can get when it comes to understanding who the authentic Jesus is.

Misconceptions

I had the opportunity to speak in a girls' unit in the Los Angeles County juvenile hall. The theme of my talk was "Who do you say Jesus really is?" When I finished, one of the girls motioned for me to come over to her table. "Y'all think this Jesus is Lord and King. But I know better," she blurted out. "He ain't nothing but one of the boys in the 'hood. He's just like the other boys hustlin' for a piece of the action on my street." This girl had no clue who Jesus really is, and yet He's the only one who can help her straighten her life out.

On another occasion I was speaking to a group of youth pastors and youth workers at a training seminar called "Reaching Today's Teens." As we discussed the most effective ways to tell teenagers about Jesus, I reminded the audience how important it is not to reduce the Lord to someone less than who He really is. In our attempts to show how Jesus can relate to students, we have gone too far with things like "Jesus the thrasher" or even "The goth Jesus." The Jesus of the Bible goes beyond all that and is already totally relevant to the lives of teenagers today.

One youth pastor spoke up and said that he totally disagreed with what I was saying. He explained that the only Jesus the kids in his neighborhood would accept is "Jesus the homeboy." And before he could even share Jesus with his kids, he needed to help them feel good about themselves culturally.

I couldn't believe what I was hearing. No wonder it's so hard for some people to understand who Jesus really is! This guy had it all backwards, sideways, and totally messed up. Jesus isn't a metal head, a thrasher, or a homeboy. He's the Son of God, the Lord of Lords, and the King of Kings. And no matter what our age, the only way we will feel good about ourselves is when we find our true identity in Christ. (We'll talk more about this later.)

Maybe you've already come to the conclusion that Jesus is more than a homeboy, but have you surrendered to Him as Lord of your life? One of the most important things you need to survive the attacks of the devil and the forces of darkness is to know and understand the Jesus of the Bible. When you are able to submit to the authority of Jesus, you will be able to stand up to the schemes and attacks of the Evil One.

WHO IS JESUS?

Jesus is still the most controversial person who has ever lived. For centuries people have been confused about Him and still are today. Try asking people at school or in your neighborhood "Who do you think Jesus is?" and you'll get lots of different answers. This is the most crucial question in life. Our answer will spell the difference between life and death, the difference between a meaningful life and a meaningless one.

Jesus asked this very question of his followers. Let's look at the answers He got. In Matthew 16:13–16 is the following discussion:

> When Jesus came to the region of Caesarea Philippi, he asked his disciples, "Who do people say that the Son of Man is?" "Well," they replied, "some say John the Baptist, some say Elijah, and others say Jeremiah or one of the other prophets."
> Then he asked them, "But who do you say I am?" Simon Peter answered, "You are the Messiah, the Son of the living God."

At first the disciples answered Jesus' question with the common view people had—that Jesus was one of the great prophets who had been brought back to life. However, Peter acknowledges Jesus as the promised and long-awaited Messiah. If Jesus were to ask you this question, how would you answer? Is He your Savior and Lord?

To live the kind of life God designed for us and to survive Satan's attacks, there are two things that we all have to be absolutely sure about: We have to know who Jesus is, and we also have to know what He did.

WHAT DİD JESUS DO?

Two thousand years ago Jesus entered the human race. He was born in a barn in a small Jewish town to a working-class family. He never wrote a book, got married, or went to college. Jesus never traveled more than two hundred miles from his birthplace and lived only to be thirty-three years old. Yet despite His rather humble existence, Jesus lived the most influential life of anyone ever.

Jesus was both completely God and completely man. His life was distinct, with things that entirely set Him apart from anyone else.

No one has ever said what Jesus said. He claimed that He was God (John 8:19; 10:30; 14:9). He also said that He had the authority to forgive sins for eternity (Mark 2:1–12), and that He was the only way to God (John 14:6).

No one has ever lived like Jesus lived. He was born of a virgin (Matthew 1:20), had no home as an adult, and had no income. He healed the sick and gave sight to the blind (Mark 1:33–34; John 9). His life was perfect and without sin (Hebrews 4:15). He suffered unjust opposition, an unfair trial, and undeserved execution. And He lived to give us life abundantly and eternally (John 10:10, 28). Jesus Christ was the perfect model for the rest of humanity in what it means to be totally dependent on God. No one can ever say to God, "You don't understand." He has experienced and been through it all. Some might argue that Buddha, Marx, and Muhammad also lived similar lives, but none could truly compare with the life of Jesus.

Nobody in all of history has ever had the influence of Jesus. More than one-third of the people in the world admit to being followers of His. Without a doubt He is the greatest person who has ever lived. While he was imprisoned on the island of St. Helena, Napoleon had this to say about Jesus:

> Alexander, Caesar, Charlemagne and myself have founded great empires, but on what did those creations of our genius rest? Upon force. But Jesus founded his on love. This very day millions would die for him. I have inspired multitudes with enthusiastic devotion: they would die for me. But to do it, I had to be present with the electric influence of my looks, my words, my voice. When I saw men and spoke to them I lit up the flame of devotion in their hearts. But Jesus Christ by some mysterious influence, even through the lapse of eighteen centuries, so draws the hearts of men towards him that thousands at a word would rush through fire and flood for him, not counting their lives dear to themselves.[1]

Certainly, Muhammad also had a great influence. But his lifestyle was very different from Jesus'. From its beginning, Muhammad's religion, Islam, was militaristic. He attacked passing caravans for their valuables and wiped out the Jewish tribe of Banu Quraiza after the battle of Khandaq in AD 627. Although there are some exceptions of moderate, peace-loving Islamic countries, in many parts of the world today Islam remains a religion of force. A vivid demonstration is the 9/11 attacks on the World Trade Center towers and the Pentagon. Some might argue that there have been representatives of Christianity who have also committed some horrible acts, but not its Founder. Jesus refused the way of force and embraced the way of love. Besides His inspiration for purity, care for others, and generosity, the greatest example of Jesus' life of love was His death on the cross. It was self-sacrificing, unconditional love for His enemies.

No one has ever taught like Jesus taught. He taught as one who had authority and not like the religious teachers of the day (Matthew 7:29). Jesus never quoted any authority other than Scripture. His teaching was deep and powerful. But look at some of the other things that made Jesus' teaching unique:

+ He never taught anything incorrect.
+ The wisdom He taught with was awesome, yet He had little formal education.
+ No one has ever been able to improve on His moral teachings.
+ His teaching is relevant to all people in every culture.

Jesus' behavior also matched his teaching, something never equaled. Confucius, Muhammad, Buddha, and even Mother Teresa all taught some good things. None of these great leaders ever managed to carry out what they taught. But Jesus taught the highest standards that any teacher has ever put together, and He kept them all.

Jesus would suffer many things and would be crucified on a cross. But His death on the cross would be different from others (Mark 8:31). Jesus suffered the punishment we deserved; He took on the sins of the world (Isaiah 53:6). Jesus dealt with human evil as no other religious leader ever has.

Human evil just won't go away. It's been around since the

very first man and woman. Just look around you—on your campus, on TV, in a newspaper, or maybe even in your own family; it's everywhere. Jesus is the only one who has answers to the problem of human evil—it's a heart problem. Jeremiah 17:9 puts it this way: "The human heart is the most deceitful of all things, and desperately wicked. Who really knows how bad it is?" People just don't have good hearts, contrary to what some religions want us to believe.

Because God is holy, He must judge evil. The consequence for sin—evil—is death (Romans 6:23). On the other hand, because God is love, He reaches out to the offender in a powerful way. "But God demonstrates his own love for us in this: While we were still sinners, Christ died for us" (Romans 5:8 NIV). God did more than deal with human evil rightly: He paid the penalty for it himself. Christ offered a single sacrifice, for all time and for everyone who would ever live. Jesus, like no other religious teacher or leader, offers complete forgiveness and a brand-new life.

And no one ever rose from the dead as Jesus did. After His death, His body was placed in a tomb, which was sealed (Mark 15:46–47). Three days later His followers went to the tomb and found it empty (Matthew 28:5–7). After His resurrection, Jesus showed himself to many people and gave them convincing proof that He was alive (Acts 1:3). Jesus was brought back to life in time and space by the supernatural power of God. By conquering death, Jesus proved He was who He claimed to be. This becomes the major reason why we should believe the Christian view of heaven and hell over Islam, Buddhism, Hinduism, or any other religion.

It was one thing for Jesus to make promises about life after death, but it was a whole different issue for Him to validate this claim by rising from the dead after three days. The evidence for

His resurrection is powerful. Muhammad died at sixty-two and did nothing to validate his claims about life after death. He remained dead, and his bones still lie in Medina. Buddha's bones were divided up and are currently enshrined in several different countries. The tomb of Jesus is empty, and His bones are not found in a memorial somewhere to be viewed. Jesus is alive, and His resurrection is what began the entire Christian movement. Because Jesus is alive, we can know Him personally and enjoy a relationship with Him in this life, and we can be confident of spending eternity with Him. Jesus has changed my life, and He can change yours as well.

JESUS DEFEATED SATAN

We can have confidence in Jesus and victory in spiritual warfare because He defeated Satan through His life, death, and resurrection. Jesus is not only our protector, He's also the greatest conqueror ever!

Jesus defeated Satan through His life

A prime example of this is found in Matthew 4:1–11:

> Then Jesus was led by the Spirit into the wilderness to be tempted there by the devil. For forty days and forty nights he fasted and became very hungry. During that time the devil came and said to him, "If you are the Son of God, tell these stones to become loaves of bread." But Jesus told him, "No! The Scriptures say, 'People do not live by bread alone, but by every word that comes from the mouth of God.'"
>
> Then the devil took him to the holy city, Jerusalem, to the highest point of the Temple, and said, "If you are the Son of God, jump off! For the Scriptures say, 'He will order his angels to protect you. And they will hold you up with their hands so

you won't even hurt your foot on a stone.' "

Jesus responded, "The Scriptures also say, 'You must not test the Lord your God.' "

Next the devil took him to the peak of a very high mountain and showed him all the kingdoms of the world and their glory. "I will give it all to you," he said, "if you will kneel down and worship me."

"Get out of here, Satan," Jesus told him. "For the Scriptures say, 'You must worship the Lord your God and serve only him.' "

Then the devil went away, and angels came and took care of Jesus.

Satan tempted Jesus in three main ways: physical, spiritual, and psychological. First, Jesus was enticed to meet His physical needs apart from God. Living independent of God is sin. Satan wanted Jesus to trust in himself and not rely on anyone else—including God.

In the second temptation, Satan dared Jesus to test God. But Jesus knew that even though the devil supported his temptation with Scripture, he was only quoting part of the passage from Psalm 91:11–12. Satan left out the most important part, which tells us that the angels will help to keep us from stumbling in the first place. Jesus also knew that exposing yourself to danger needlessly is a way of testing God, and this goes against the principle of faith we are to live by.

In the third temptation, the devil offered Jesus all the kingdoms of the world—if Jesus would just worship him. Satan psychologically tempted Jesus with power. But Jesus knew that God is the only one who should be worshiped and served.

Jesus was able to stand up to the devil—against every temptation—by living a life in obedience to God and His Word. The way Jesus lived His life gave Him the ability to defeat Satan. And the same can be true for us. It all comes back to knowing the Bible and obeying it.

Jesus defeated Satan through His death

From the time of Christ's birth, Satan did all in his power to bring about Jesus' downfall. But he was doomed to fail. The Bible says in 1 John 3:8, "The Son of God came to destroy the works of the devil." This happened through Christ's death on the cross and His resurrection. He took on the sins of the world and suffered the punishment that we deserved (Isaiah 53:6). He was our substitute so we could be forgiven. Jesus died our death so we could live.

On the cross, Jesus destroyed the fear of death, which Satan has used to enslave people. In Hebrews 2:14–15 we read about Christ's destruction of the devil's hold on us:

> Because God's children are human beings—made of flesh and blood—the Son also became flesh and blood. For only as a human being could he die, and only by dying could he break the power of the devil, who had the power of death. Only in this way could he set free all who have lived their lives as slaves to the fear of dying.

Satan and his demonic army have been mortally wounded; they're going down for the count! And for those who trust in Christ, eternal life is guaranteed and we don't have to be afraid of dying when it happens. All of this and more is a result of Jesus' death on the cross.

Jesus defeated Satan through His resurrection

By far the greatest thing that is unique about Jesus is His resurrection. It is the most important part of the Gospel.

After Jesus' body was taken off the cross, it was placed in a borrowed tomb. Three days later He was raised. Christianity stands or falls on the resurrection of Jesus Christ. The Bible puts it this way: "If there is no resurrection of the dead, then Christ has not been raised either. And if Christ has not been raised, then all our preaching is useless, and your faith is useless" (1 Corinthians 15:13–14).

The word *resurrection* in the Bible is defined as "the standing up of a body." The resurrection of Jesus was not only spiritual but physical. Jesus' body literally "stood up" from the grave back to life. When the Bible says Jesus gave "convincing proof" He was alive, it was speaking of physical life, not just some "spirit being" or ghost walking around.

According to many scholars, there is no historic event better supported by the evidence than the resurrection of Jesus Christ. The fact that Jesus actually died and rose from the grave confirms His uniqueness and proves that He is the Son of God. No one else in history has ever been able to predict his own resurrection and then fulfill it. The fact of the empty tomb was not the result of some scheme to make His resurrection plausible. Any attempt to disprove it is met head-on with mounds of evidence, beginning with Christ's documented appearances.

After His resurrection, Jesus appeared many times to different people. Taking the books Matthew, Mark, Luke, and John into account, here's a chronological order of the Lord's appearances:

+ Resurrection Sunday: To Mary Magdalene (John 20:14–18); the women coming back from the tomb with the angel's message (Matthew 28:8–10); in the afternoon to Peter (Luke 24:34; 1 Corinthians 15:5); toward evening to the disciples on the road to Emmaus (Luke 24:13–31); all the apostles except Thomas (Luke 24:36–43; John 20:19–24).

+ Eight days later: To the apostles, including Thomas (John 20:26–29).

+ In Galilee: At the Lake of Tiberias to the seven (John 21:1–23); to the apostles and more than five hundred others (1 Corinthians 15:5–6).

+ At Jerusalem and Bethany (a second time): To James (1 Corinthians 15:7); to the eleven (Matthew 28:16–20; Mark 16:14–20; Luke 24:33–53; Acts 1:3–12).

+ To Paul: Near Damascus (Acts 9:3–6; 1 Corinthians 15:8); in the temple (Acts 22:17–21; 23:11).

+ To Stephen: Outside Jerusalem (Acts 7:55).

+ To John: On the island of Patmos (Revelation 1:10–19).

Stop for a minute. Let the evidence you've just read sink in. Jesus appeared only to His followers. For the most part His appearances were infrequent, with only four after Easter and before His return back to heaven. There was nothing fantastic or weird about His appearances, and they were all different in nature—in the places they occurred, the length of time involved, the words spoken, and even the mood of the apostles. All Christ's appearances were physical because Jesus wanted the disciples to be sure of this fact (Luke 24:39–40; John 20:27).

It's absolutely incredible to think that so many people, on different days and in distinct situations, had encounters with the risen Christ. The resurrection of Christ means that God gave His approval to the claims and works of Jesus. These claims would have been blasphemous if Jesus were not truly the Son of God. However, the resurrection validates Jesus and His teaching. The empty tomb should assure us forever that all the things He taught were true. If Christ had not risen from the dead, then He wouldn't be alive to do all His post-resurrection work. We would not have an Advocate, our Defender. Ultimately, there'd be no supernatural person to live inside us and give us power (Romans 6:1–10; Galatians 2:20).

Jesus was brought back to life in time and space by the supernatural power of God as proof that He is exactly who He says He is, and so that we would be acceptable to God in spite of our own sin (Romans 4:25).

In His death Jesus took away our sins, and in His resurrection He gave us a guaranteed entrance to heaven and unlimited power to face the problems of life. Because of the resurrection we have hope. And this hope gives meaning and purpose to life. So many people today lack direction for their lives because they don't know Jesus. Life without Christ is a hopeless end; life with Christ is an endless hope.

The good news is that this same power is available to you and me to help us face the struggles and overcome the pain of life. Jesus Christ is alive and is able to meet all your needs.

WHERE OUR VICTORY COMES FROM

Even though Satan is a defeated foe, the spiritual battle will continue until the day we exit this life and go to be with Jesus. Victory in the battle can be ours by daily submitting to Jesus and acknowledging Him as Lord of our lives.

When you go to a doctor for medical care, you submit yourself to him or her. You may not always agree with what the doctor says or prescribes, but you obey him or her—most of the time! You take the medicine, even if it tastes gross, because the doctor is the boss at that moment, and he or she knows what's best.

To submit to Christ means we must willfully surrender to God and take a stand against the devil. It means we want God's desires for our life more than we want our own way. Instead of resisting God's will for us, we should resist the devil. We acknowledge Jesus as Lord (the boss) because He created us and knows what's best for us.

If we submit to God and resist the devil, the Bible says Satan will flee from us (James 4:7). The devil can be resisted. Jesus was our example, and it is by His resurrection power that we can stand up against Satan and not give in to temptation.

Make it a priority to spend time each day developing and growing in your relationship with Jesus. Get to know the "real thing" so that when the counterfeit—our Enemy—attacks, you will recognize him. Dig in and study God's Word, especially the first four books of the New Testament—Matthew, Mark, Luke, and John. These books give us a great picture of who Jesus is, what He is like, and how He relates to people.

When you get to know Jesus, you can't help but love Him. And the more you love Him, the more you'll want to please Him. The closer you get to Jesus and live the truth, the more easily you will see the lie that Satan is trying to make you believe. But all this takes time, and you'll have to make some changes in the way you think and the way you live.

Think about other relationships in your life. If you never spent any time with your friends and family, what kind of relationships would you have? You know those people because you spend time with them. And the same is true with Jesus. Take time to get to know Jesus now before the devil really starts turning up the heat. It's the most important thing you could ever do.

Jesus isn't like any other religious leader. He's the Son of God and your Defender. Jesus is on your side and wants you to win at life. Think about it: If God is for us, who can be against us? (Romans 8:31).

THINK ABOUT IT

1. What is the difference between knowing about Jesus and having an intimate knowledge of Him? Be specific.

2. Who first told you about Jesus? How was He described to you? What about Him did you find appealing at first? What about now?

3. What areas of your life are the most difficult to submit to God? Why?

4. What temptation(s) is the devil putting before you? What changes do you need to make so you will be able to stand up to the devil and experience victory in the spiritual battle?

CHAPTER 12

WHO ARE YOU?

Can you remember back to when you were just a little kid? Who were your heroes? What were your favorite books? One of my favorites was the story of Peter Pan. I always liked it when my Mom would read about Peter, Wendy, and Captain Hook, although I have to admit that Captain Hook used to scare me when I was a really small guy! I enjoyed watching the movie version because the story came alive! It was a fun fantasy. My younger brother and sister and I even liked to make believe that we would travel to Neverland on our backyard swing set. Then I remember the first time we went to Disneyland. My brother, sister, and I could hardly wait to go on all the rides—especially the Peter Pan ride in Fantasyland!

Fast-forward with me now that I'm a big guy. I got hold of a DVD copy of a back-listed movie called *Hook*. It turned out to be a contemporary version of Peter Pan, this time taking place in the 1990s. Peter Pan is a grown-up now and is known as Chief Executive Officer Peter Banning. He has all the stuff that a CEO possesses: expensive cars, power suits, expense accounts, and the latest in high-tech toys. His life is so wrapped up in the corporate world that he doesn't have a whole lot of time for his family or even himself.

Peter, his wife, and their two children make a trip to England to visit Granny Wendy, the woman who raised him. A new wing of a children's home is going to be named in her honor, and there's a special dinner being held in tribute to Granny Wendy.

On the night of the banquet, Peter's son and daughter are

kidnapped. The abductor tacks a note onto the door of the children's room with a big dagger. The message is from the evil Captain Hook, challenging Peter to the ultimate duel over his children in Neverland.

Peter Banning soon faces a double crisis: His children are gone and Granny Wendy tells him that he must come to grips with his true identity—he's really Peter Pan—to rescue his children. But Peter rebels against this new knowledge because he doesn't want to accept who he really is.

Tinkerbell then visits Peter in the middle of the night and carries him off to Neverland. He experiences a fascinating adventure, but he's also working through a tremendous identity crisis. Tinkerbell and the Lost Boys tell Peter that he must try to remember who he really is, and the only way this will happen is by recalling a happy memory. His happy memory finally comes to him—it's when he became a father for the first time.

Suddenly, Peter's life is totally transformed. He now believes and understands who he really is, and his life takes on new meaning and purpose. Peter is able to defeat Captain Hook and rescue his children. All of them eventually return home together from Neverland and live happily ever after.

Do you really know who you are? Are you struggling with an identity crisis of your own? This is another area of spiritual warfare that we sometimes fail to recognize. If the devil can keep us confused about our true identity, he'll keep us frustrated and lacking confidence, and we will not become the person God designed us to be.

Knowing who you are is the key to a meaningful life. When we come to grips with this, our whole perspective on life radically changes. But many people don't know how to find their identity—it takes more than a happy memory—and when they do, they oftentimes don't want to believe it. They're afraid they might have to become someone they don't really want to be.

HOW *NOT* TO DETERMINE WHO YOU ARE

Telling me your name, where you live or go to school, and what you like to do are things about you. But even with all that information, you still haven't told me who you really are.

Who we are is not determined by what we do, where we live or go to school, or even the things we possess. I remember meeting a high school guy who introduced himself to me and immediately told me about the brand-new Mustang convertible his dad had just bought him. This guy went on and on about his car for more than twenty minutes. He told me every detail imaginable!

I wanted to jump in and interrupt him: "Time out! Are you trying to tell me who you are or are you telling me about something you own? There seems to be some confusion here."

When I was in high school I did well in academics and sports, but my passion was music—playing the drums. It was my life. So when I went to my high school class reunion, people thought I was still doing the music gig. They would come up to me and say, "Hey, Russo. What's happening? Who are you playing with now?" When I responded that I was now in full-time ministry, they didn't know what to do with me. It was almost as if I had told them I had some strange, highly contagious tropical disease. They politely said good-bye and took off to another part of the room. During all those years in school everyone had my identity wrapped up in the drums. And so did I.

The misconception over identity can work the opposite way too. If you can't perform or you don't have the status or bling the world says you need—lies from the devil—you begin to think of yourself as worthless. You can see yourself as a loser because you didn't make good grades in a particular class or you didn't make a certain team. Or maybe you have been hearing for a long time from your parents, teachers, or friends that you'll never succeed in anything.

I took a speech class my freshman year of college, and one day after class the professor asked to speak to me privately. "There's one thing I want to encourage you never to consider as a profession," she said. "Public speaking. You just don't have what it takes." That's funny, isn't it? Today I speak to groups all over the world, plus on radio and TV! I'd like to find that professor now and let her know what God can do in a person's life.

Have you discovered your identity? Do you really know who you are? Who you are is determined by much more than what you have, what you do, and what you achieve.

DISCOVERIΠG WHO YOU ARE

As far back as he could remember, Keith Wegeman's main goal in life was to make the Olympic ski team. Finally, in 1952, he was chosen for the ski jump. After months of practice, Keith headed to Europe for the games. The day finally came when he was to experience the greatest thrill of his life. There he stood at the top of the world's highest ski jump at Oberstdorf, Germany.

For a moment he paused, all alone, 650 feet above the outrun of the jump. The eighty thousand people below seemed no bigger than ants. Then the signal was given and the crowd was silent as he plummeted down at over eighty miles per hour. His senses couldn't keep up with the scream of the wind and the blur of trees, snow, and sky. Then suddenly he was hanging motionless over the white hill below. After what seemed like an eternity, Keith landed sixteen feet beyond the four-hundred-foot mark, the longest jump an American skier had ever made up to that time.

Two months later Keith was on a plane headed back to New York. The Olympics were over. Now what? As the engines droned on endlessly, somewhere over the Atlantic it hit him: *What, then, does last? What's important? What's the answer?* He was twenty-three years old and had never thought about these questions before. Once he arrived home, he couldn't seem to find any thrills that would last—they all wore thin quickly, even the celebrity status he now had with all the endorsements and appearances.

Sometime later he was in Southern California visiting his brother and some friends, who invited him to attend a young adult's conference in the San Bernardino Mountains. He attended a few of the meetings but spent most of his time swimming, climbing, and hiking. Still, Keith decided he'd better make an appearance at the closing meeting. The meeting hall was hot, and he didn't really listen too much until the speaker was toward the end of his message and started talking about pleasures in this life that don't last. Keith sat straight up in his chair when he heard the speaker say, "What, then, *does* last? What's important in the long run? What's the answer?" He couldn't believe his ears. Those were the same questions he had asked himself while flying over the Atlantic.

"Do you want to know the answer?" the speaker continued. Keith bent forward in his chair and heard, "Try Jesus." Keith jumped up and ran outside toward the safety of the mountains. After an hour, he finally stopped, sat down on a slope, and let the words he'd been running from catch up to him. He had known about Jesus as an idea or principle, but now he would know Him as a person. Keith's life would never be the same.

Now he had a different kind of thrills to live for—ones that wouldn't wear thin.[1]

Keith learned what everyone on this planet needs to know: You become complete as a person and have a life of meaning and purpose when you find your identity in Jesus. This happens when we put our faith and trust in Him as Savior and Lord, when we decide to live our life for and like Him.

It's only in Christ that we find out who we really are. And that's what finally happened to Keith. He was confronted with and came to love the One who knew him better than anyone else, even better than he knew himself. He found out about the One who put him together, piece by piece, molecule by molecule, in his mother's womb. In Jesus his true identity was found. And this knowledge totally transformed Keith Wegeman's life.

How about you? Have you come to grips with who you are in Christ? Do you know He loves you just the way you are? You're somebody special in His eyes. Billions of people have been born and walked the face of this planet, yet there have never been any two who are exactly alike—not even identical twins. That famous author "Anonymous" wrote some words that describe this fact perfectly. After you read "I'm Special," take a minute to let the words really sink in.

I'm Special

I'm special. In all the world there's nobody like me. Since the beginning of time, there has never been another person like me. Nobody has my smile. Nobody has my eyes, my nose, my hair, my hands, my voice. I'm special.

No one can be found who has my handwriting. Nobody anywhere has my tastes for food or music or art. No one sees things just as I do. In all of time there's been no one who laughs like me, no one who cries like me. And what makes me laugh and cry will never provoke identical laughter and tears from anybody else, ever. No one reacts to any situation just as I would react. I'm special.

I'm the only one in all of creation who has my set of abilities. Oh, there will always be somebody who is better at one of the things I'm good at, but no one in the universe can reach my combination of talents, ideas, abilities and feelings. Like a room full of musical instruments, some may excel alone, but none can match the symphony sound when all are played together. I'm a symphony.

Through all of eternity no one will ever look, talk, walk, think, or do like me. I'm special. I'm rare.

And in all rarity there is great value. Because of my great rare value, I need not attempt to imitate others. I will accept—yes, celebrate—my differences. I'm special.

And I'm beginning to realize it's no accident that I'm special. I'm beginning to see that God made me special for a very special purpose.

He must have a job for me that no one else can do as well as I. Out of all the billions of applicants, only one is qualified, only one has the right combination of what it takes.

That one is me. Because . . . I'm special.

Now that you're beginning to realize just how special you are, let's take a closer look at how to begin developing your true identity.

YOUR TRUE IDENTITY

In the Bible we learn that if anyone is in Christ, he is a new creation. "The old life is gone; a new life has begun!" (2 Corinthians 5:17). When you open your heart and life to Jesus Christ, you become a brand-new person, a person who didn't exist before. The apostle Paul writes in Ephesians 5:8, "For once you were full of darkness, but now you have light from the Lord. So live as people of light!" There isn't anything more dramatically different than darkness and light. This is how different your life will be once you recognize who you are in Jesus.

Unfortunately, this concept is often misunderstood today. Let's clear up some of the confusion. To begin with, did you know that there are two births you can have in life? A physical one and a spiritual one. When we are born physically, the result is physical life. When we are "born again" spiritually, we receive eternal life.

When we are born spiritually, it opens up all the other dimensions of our life—social, emotional, physical, intellectual—enabling us to become the people God has designed us to be. That one missing piece ultimately makes sense out of life. A new life in Christ gives you a brand-new identity. Becoming a Christian—a follower of Jesus—is not just something you add to your life; it becomes your life. You may look the same on the outside, but you are a radically different person on the inside.

As a follower of Jesus you are a brand-new person. God has given you a new heart. You have been completely forgiven of all your sins and given a new start at life. That means you can stop living under the cloud of guilt the devil is attempting to put over you about your past. Start experiencing life as the person God designed you to be. Not only has your sin debt been paid in full, but you've also been given an awesome new power to overcome the challenges in life as well.

Life isn't always easy, especially in today's world. Broken families, money problems, unrealistic expectations, abuse, and stress can get you down. Things get even more complicated when you add the spiritual battle raging in our lives. Don't get too bummed out, though. Instead, stand up to the devil and the philosophies of the world, and start enjoying life God's way!

In Jeremiah 29:11 we read, "'I know the plans I have for you,' says the Lord. 'They are plans for good and not for disaster, to give you a future and a hope.'" God wants you to get the most out of life. When you have secured your destiny and identity through Christ, it should affect the quality of life you live here on earth. There will always be problems, pressures, and struggles, but the way you respond is going to be different, because now you have all the resources of the living God changing your life and giving you power to face the challenges head on.

It's critically important to realize that you are not the same person after you surrender your life to Christ. You may be thinking to yourself, *Steve, I accepted Jesus, and I'm still struggling with my identity and self-image.* Then you've been deceived by the devil. He has distorted the truth about your identity. Stop listening to the lies of the Enemy and start living God's truth. Satan would like you to believe that you're nothing more than a rotten sinner; however, God doesn't see us as sinners but rather as saints who are struggling with sin and the temptations of this world (Ephesians 1). This is part of our new identity.

God changes us so completely in Jesus that even He looks at us differently. The Bible teaches that we are God's workmanship created in Christ Jesus to do good works, which God prepared in advance for us to do (Ephesians 2:10). God designed us to do good things—to win at life!

Meaning and purpose in life that last cannot be found outside of Jesus. Stop chasing the empty bubbles that Satan is blowing in your path. You are a child of God. Live in an appropriate way. John 1:12 tells us, "To all who believed him and accepted him, he gave the right to become children of God." Since Christ is the Lord of Lords and the King of Kings, what does that make us? We're children of the King. Talk about significant! There's nothing that even comes close! Are you living like the royalty you really are?

Paul, in Ephesians 4:1, puts it another way: "I, a prisoner for serving the Lord, beg you to lead a life worthy of your calling, for you have been called by God." What happens when Prince Charles of England goes anywhere? How is he treated? People literally roll out the red carpet for him. Heads of state and bands greet him. People take extra special care of him. He even has bodyguards. Why? Because he is the son of royalty and the future king of England.

But just think: If you have put your faith and trust in Jesus, you have a much greater heritage and inheritance than Prince Charles. You are a child of the King of the heavens and will rule forever with the Lord of all creation.

How God describes who we are in Christ

The Bible is filled with incredible descriptions of our identity in Jesus Christ. Let's take a look at some of the verses that can help us get an even better idea of who we really are.

In 1 Corinthians 6:19–20 we read: "Don't you realize that your body is the temple of the Holy Spirit, who lives in you and was given to you by God? You do not belong to yourself, for God bought you with a high price." What was the cost of buying our freedom from the powers of darkness? It was the very life of God's only Son, Jesus. God paid the highest price possible so our relationship with Him could be restored and our true identity secured. Isn't it amazing how valuable we are to God and how much He loves us?

Knowing that we were bought with such a tremendous price should cause us to be more careful in the things we get involved with. You don't have to "loan yourself out" and sell out your values to things like sex before marriage, gangs, cutting, or even abusing drugs and alcohol just to feel worth something. There's no longer any reason to compromise to get someone to love you. God cares about you and will provide for all your needs—even when it comes to relationships. You were bought with the ultimate price, so live like it and don't settle for anything less.

Colossians 1:13 describes the security that is part of our identity: "He has rescued us from the kingdom of darkness and transferred us into the Kingdom of his dear Son." Before we accepted Christ, you and I were hostages of the devil to do his will (2 Timothy 2:26). We were prisoners, but God set us free! And Jesus said that once we were His, no one could take us from Him (John 10:28).

Check out the words of Jesus in Luke 15:7: "There is more joy in heaven over one lost sinner who repents and returns to God than over ninety-nine others who are righteous and haven't strayed away!" When someone surrenders their life to Jesus Christ, it's party time in heaven! Spiritual freedom is secure and lasts forever.

Next time you're feeling insecure because friends have rejected you or you have a tough family situation, stop and think about your security in Christ. Let this knowledge about your true identity influence your behavior. There's no need to fear anyone or anything that life may throw at you. The Bible says that "God has not given us a spirit of fear . . . but of power, love, and self-discipline" (2 Timothy 1:7). Having a relationship with Jesus really can make a difference in the way you live.

Isn't it incredible how many dimensions of life our identity (or lack of it) affects?

With Jesus we have everything we'll ever need to make life worth living. That's not to say we don't need other relationships or a fulfilling career, but without knowing who we are in Christ, they are meaningless. Ephesians 1:3 says that we have been blessed with every spiritual blessing. Our minds can't even begin to comprehend what God has blessed us with or what He has planned for us (1 Corinthians 2:9). Don't miss what you already have in Jesus by continuing to search for something more in all the wrong places.

KNOWING WHO WE ARE AFFECTS HOW WE ACT

The more I think about what our identity in Christ means in our day-to-day lives, the more convinced I am that we can see some of the problems that plague us today shrink and disappear altogether.

For example, "hooking up" or "friends with benefits"—the teen sex crisis. Every year three million teenagers (one out of four) get sexually transmitted diseases, including AIDS, gonorrhea, and HPV. Chlamydia is more common among teens than among older men and women. Schools are passing out condoms on campus (perhaps on yours?), but it isn't helping deal with the root of the problem. Teens are having sex because they want to feel loved, accepted, and significant. And they're attempting to gain all those things through a physical relationship.

Sex outside of marriage only causes scars and emotional pain. Satan lies and says it will make you feel loved and accepted—and will even keep a relationship together. But it won't. Sex is a very special gift from God for married couples, and it's being misused with tragic results in our society. I'm convinced that if you and your peers understand who you are in Christ—that you're secure, accepted, and significant—fewer of you will decide to be sexually active. In Christ, you can have a confidence in yourself that can help you not give in to the pressures of sexual temptation.

Another problem caused by the identity crisis is drug and alcohol abuse. Alcohol-related traffic deaths are still one of the top three killers of teenagers each year. Why do people drink and do drugs? Sometimes to get others to like them and to feel accepted. Other times it's a way of dealing with the pain and disappointment in life. But there's a better way to handle pain. Jesus gives us a promise in Matthew 11:28: "Come to me, all of you who are weary and carry heavy burdens, and I will give you rest."

Once again, if you and other students could grab hold of who you really are in Jesus Christ and all that God has designed you to be and experience, we'd see this problem of drug and alcohol abuse greatly decrease.

Bullying has become a huge problem in schools today. I'm sure you've seen kids pick on other kids or harass them because of religion, race, looks, or speech. Bullying takes the following forms: verbal, hitting, pushing, or slapping; spreading rumors; and making sexual comments or gestures. Almost a third of teens are either bullies or have been bullied. Some people become bullies because they are insecure, while others have been abused or hurt by somebody in the past. Some bullying has even turned deadly.

Or how about the explosive problem with gangs throughout the country? This used to be confined to the big city, but no more. Now, whether it's the Bloods and the Crips or the Trench Coat Mafia, gangs are everywhere. And gangs will accept almost anyone. Gang members are in search of a sense of family, acceptance, security, and love. They may find these things with the gang, but it's only temporary. It still doesn't get to the root of the problem: the need for a relationship with Christ.

The answer to the gang problem is to help students from all walks of life and every color understand who they can be in Jesus

Christ and how to come to grips with their true identity—
which includes being part of God's forever family.

I could fill pages with crises from the youth culture—your
culture—that find their roots in the identity issue. We could talk
about eating disorders, suicidal tendencies, and people who cut
themselves, and we'd keep coming back to the fact that knowing
who we are affects how we act. I don't want to sound overly
simplistic, but so many problems today could be solved by helping people find their true identity and letting that influence the
way they live.

The only place you are going to find your real identity is in
an intimate relationship with Jesus Christ. This happens by surrendering your heart and life to Him and saying, "Jesus, I want
you to invade my humanity and help me to become the person
I was designed to be so I can live my life to the fullest."

Some of the most frequent questions students ask me as I
travel are, "Can you give me a reason to get up in the morning?"
"Why am I here?" "How do I make my life count?" All of these
and more can be answered in one word—Jesus. Satan will try to
deceive you into not believing this awesome truth. The Enemy
started doing this back in the beginning of human history with
the first man and woman, and he hasn't changed his strategy
since. Deception is his greatest weapon, especially when it comes
to our identity. Satan knows all too well that the truth about
who you are is the one thing that will set you free. Jesus said, "I
am the way, the truth, and the life" (John 14:6). Lasting security,
acceptance, and significance will only be found in Christ.

Find yourself in Him and your life will never be the same.
And remember this simple truth: Satan has come to take from
you; Jesus has come to give to you.

THINK ABOUT IT

1. How do you find your true identity? Read John 3:1–3.
2. Take a three-by-five card and write the following on it: "I am a child of the King." Then put this card someplace where you will see it several times each day—on your dresser, in your locker, or on a mirror. This will be a small reminder of your true identity.
3. Have you ever felt inadequate and wished you were someone else? Why? How could understanding your true identity help in this situation?
4. What does it mean to live your life for or like Jesus?

CHAPTER 13

COMBAT READY

A professional soldier's success in battle depends on his preparation and his equipment. It would be suicidal to step into the heat of combat ill-equipped and unprepared. Tragically, many Christians today have not yet realized that we are also soldiers in the most intensive and crucial battle ever fought. Each day we face a brutal and fierce enemy. Many times we stumble home beaten up, wounded, and discouraged because we have not prepared ourselves for battle.

The battle in the student's world includes physical and sexual abuse, emotional hurt, loneliness, stress, lack of purpose and direction, drug and alcohol abuse, premarital sex, abortion, broken families, eating disorders, and gangs. It's not easy to grow up in a world of confusing messages that kick you when you're down.

And the one who is behind so much of this pain is relentless. The devil doesn't want to let go. His ultimate objective is to devour and destroy us (John 10:10; 1 Peter 5:8). But before you start feeling too overwhelmed, remember that Jesus mortally wounded Satan and the dark powers and authorities by the cross (Colossians 2:15). We need to be encouraged, knowing that Jesus is the victor and that Satan's future demise is not in doubt (Matthew 25:41; Revelation 20:10).

God has made it possible for us not only to protect ourselves from the Evil One's attacks but also to have victory in the spiritual battle. We can successfully face conflict with the devil. In Ephesians 6, the apostle Paul gives us a detailed description of the "battle gear" God has given us. This gear can withstand every spiritual attack and is all the protection we need to defend ourselves from Satan and his evil schemes. But we need to remember that we can't rely on our own power; instead, we must depend upon God's presence and His might.

Paul lived during the time of the Roman Empire, and he used the image of a Roman soldier as his model when he wrote to the church at Ephesus. The secret to the success of these seemingly invincible Roman warriors was in their preparation and their armor. In much the same way, God wants us to learn the importance of preparing for our battles by putting on our spiritual armor:

> Therefore put on the full armor of God, so that when the day of evil comes, you may be able to stand your ground, and after you have done everything, to stand. Stand firm then, with the belt of truth buckled around your waist, with the breastplate of righteousness in place, and with your feet fitted with the readiness that comes from the gospel of peace. In addition to all this, take up the shield of faith, with which you can extinguish all the flaming arrows of the evil one. Take the helmet of salvation and the sword of the Spirit, which is the word of God. And pray in the Spirit on all occasions with all kinds of prayers and requests. With this in mind, be alert and always keep on praying for all the saints. (Ephesians 6:13–18 NIV)

Let's look more closely at each piece of the armor and see how it applies to our daily life.

BELT OF TRUTH

The first piece of equipment Paul mentions is the belt. The soldier's belt, usually made of leather, belonged to the tunic he wore under his armor rather than to the armor itself, yet it was still an essential part of his equipment. It gathered his tunic together so an enemy couldn't grab it, and it also held his sword in place. Buckling it on gave him a sense of strength and confidence. He was prepared for action.

The Christian soldier's belt is truth. We need to be convinced of the truth of the Bible and what it affirms in our lives as children of God. This means we need to have a genuine commitment to Christ and truthfulness. Hypocrisy, lying, and deceit have no place in the life of a follower of Christ. Our lives should be characterized by integrity and sincerity.

The devil is the Father of Lies and uses many schemes to mislead, deceive, and trick. The bottom line is that we need to know whom we believe in and what we believe. Are you absolutely convinced that Jesus is the Son of God? Do you know what you believe about Him? Do you know the basics of your faith? Is your behavior a reflection of the truth of God's Word? If you are not certain, you're already defeated.

Make sure you are clear on who Jesus is and what the Bible teaches. It's not enough just to believe. Make sure you live God's truth. Let His truth direct your thoughts and desires, your speech, and the way you live. Remember, if Satan can get you to believe a lie, no matter how small, he can get you to live it. God's truth helps us to overcome Satan's lies.

Do you know what you believe? Could you defend your faith in a reasonable way to one of your teachers or to a skeptical relative? Do you really believe that God wants the best for you? Keep the belt of God's truth firmly buckled in your life.

BODY ARMOR OF RIGHTEOUSNESS

The soldier's second piece of armor was the breastplate. It was often made of heavy leather or strong metal and shaped to fit a

soldier's upper body, usually front and back. The breastplate protected the vital organs (heart, lungs, and intestines) from the
enemy's weapons.

During the apostle Paul's time, people thought the heart represented the mind and will, while the intestines represented the
emotions and feelings. The mind and the emotions are the two
areas where the devil most fiercely attacks Christians. He tempts
us to think wrong thoughts and feel wrong emotions. Satan
wants to cloud our thinking with false teaching and confuse our
emotions with perverted morals and loyalties.

To protect ourselves against these attacks of the Enemy, we
must put on the body armor of righteousness. Our heart must
be protected so that we can respond to our circumstances on the
basis of biblical truth. Satan tries to convince us that God could
not possibly forgive us for some of the horrible things we've
done in the past. He wants us to believe we are worthless in the
sight of God. Nothing could be further from the truth.

The righteousness that protects us from Satan comes from
Jesus, not from ourselves. It's His complete purity and perfection
before God. It is the knowledge that we have been completely
forgiven of all sin and guilt. We are accepted by God as His
friends and, even more important, as His sons and daughters
because of our relationship with Christ.

This is our primary defense against the slanderous attacks of
the Evil One. We can live confidently and boldly without guilt,
fear, and hopelessness. Having this righteousness also brings with
it responsibility. God supplies the standard and the necessary
power for right living, but we must be willing to obey Him and
His Word on a daily basis. Failure to do this ultimately results in
defeat in the spiritual battle.

Do you live by what's convenient or by what's right at home,
on your campus, or at work? If Jesus truly is our Commander in

Chief, we must take a stand for what is right, even when the wrong is the politically correct thing to do. Continue to put the righteousness of Jesus in your life by obeying Him rather than following those around you.

The Bible is filled with many examples of how God rewards obedience. It's the best defense against the slanderous attacks of the devil.

THE SHOES OF PEACE

Next on the list of the soldier's equipment is the footgear. The Roman legionnaire wore leather half boots with open toes. They had heavily spiked or studded soles and were tied to the ankles and shins with long straps. These shoes equipped him for lengthy marches and prevented his feet from slipping and sliding during battle, giving him a solid stance.

A Christian soldier without the shoes of peace is almost sure to stumble, fall, and suffer defeat at the hands of the Enemy. We need to stand on the solid foundation of the Gospel. These shoes function in two ways. First, through our relationship with Jesus Christ, we have complete peace with God. And because we are at peace with God, we can also be at peace with others and ourselves, giving us the firmest foothold possible from which to fight evil. We can stand in confidence, knowing that God loves us and that He is committed to fight for us.

Second, the Christian soldier's shoes indicate a readiness to move forward and share the good news with others. We need to be prepared to share the message of God's love and forgiveness for sin, whenever and wherever He gives us the opportunity— at homes, on campus, on the job, in our communities. The devil hates and fears the Gospel because he knows it is God's power to rescue people from his rule.

Are you prepared to stand up to the devil? Only the foundation of the Gospel and experiencing God's peace can give you the firm footing you need.

THE SHIELD OF FAITH

The shield was an indispensable part of the soldier's equipment. In Paul's day, the shield was oblong and approximately four and a half feet high and two and a half feet wide, essentially covering the entire body. It was made of two layers of wood glued together and then covered with a layer of cloth and a layer of animal hide. It was framed with a strip of iron on the top and bottom. This huge shield was uniquely designed to put out and deflect flaming arrows.

The shield of faith is essential protection for Christian soldiers, an indispensable addition to the rest of our "battle gear." This shield can deflect Satan's flaming arrows of false guilt, lust, fear, lies, discouragement, greed, and jealousy.

Genuine faith grabs hold of the promises of God's Word in times of depression and doubt, temptation and trials. This shield of faith is the awesome, total protection that God gives us against Satan's attacks. It's available to us when we choose to place our faith and confidence in God as our protector.

Everyone lives by some kind of faith. We eat food, trusting that it's not been poisoned. We put our trust in cars, buses, and planes, believing that they're safe. But faith in God is much more important than the everyday faith we live by. Jesus Christ is incredibly powerful and more dependable than anything we know, because He is God and never fails.

Be careful of the devil's fiery arrows of doubt to get you to rely on yourself rather than God. You can totally depend on the Lord to protect you and provide for you in every area of your life.

HELMET OF SALVATION

The Roman soldier's helmet was usually made of a tough iron or bronze and was designed to protect the head from injury. An inside lining made of felt helped to make the weight of the helmet more bearable. Sometimes there was a hinged visor that added more frontal protection, and these helmets were often decorated with huge colorful plumes. Only an ax or hammer could pierce these heavy helmets. A soldier would never enter battle without it.

While this military helmet was designed to protect the soldier's head, the helmet of salvation is designed to protect the Christian's mind—the devil's battlefield. Satan's attacks are directed at our thoughts. He will do everything he can to cause discouragement and doubt by pointing out anything that may be negative in our lives. He wants to throw obstacles in our way to sidetrack us and confuse us. He wants us to doubt the promises in God's Word.

As you know, the heart of spiritual warfare is really a battle for the mind. God's power is the only defense we have against the Enemy and the forces of darkness. We need to be secure in our identity in Christ. We have confidence in the assurance of God's continuing work in our life and in our final "graduation day" to come. God is never going to abandon you or turn His back on you, no matter what the situation. You can count on Him always being there for you. His unlimited power is available to you to defeat anything the Enemy may throw at you.

These first five pieces of "battle gear" that God has given us have been primarily defensive weapons. Now the focus changes to equipment used for offensive warfare.

SWORD OF THE SPIRIT—THE WORD OF GOD

A battle-ready Roman soldier was always equipped defensively and offensively. Many different kinds of weapons were available, including spears and arrows, but perhaps the most powerful weapon of all was his sword. Usually this was a short two-edged dagger, which allowed the soldier to respond quickly to an attacker. Fighting would involve a close personal encounter in hand-to-hand combat. The sword was both an offensive and defensive weapon.

God has also armed Christians with a powerful sword: the Word of God—the Bible. God puts this weapon in our hands so we can use it to have direction and guidance for living, share the good news with others, and resist temptation. When Jesus was in the wilderness, he responded to each satanic temptation with, "It is written . . ." (Matthew 4:1–11 NIV).

Hebrews 4:12 says the Bible is sharper than any two-edged sword. It's sharp enough to shred the lies that Satan throws at us, and it's sharp enough to cut through the defenses of someone without Christ. Scripture pierces the human heart, soul, and spirit to convict us of our sin and change us. Only when we know the Bible and understand how practical it is for our daily lives will we be able to use the sword effectively. In the next chapter, "Choose Your Weapons," we will discuss in greater detail some ideas on how to study and apply the Bible.

When you are faced with questions about your life, where do you turn? The Bible has real answers about relationships, the future, how to get along with others, and everything else that relates to your life. It has the power to transform your life.

PRAYER

Paul concludes the list of "battle gear" with the most important piece of equipment for spiritual warfare: prayer. Equipping ourselves with God's armor can be done only through prayer.

God's power is given to Christians by a simple act of trust in

Him. This trust is most commonly demonstrated in the act of prayer. We should pray and ask God for strength to do battle as we put on each piece of armor daily in preparation. Our armor is strengthened through consistent prayer as we tap in to the awesome power of God. Paul also reminds us to pray for our brothers and sisters in Christ in their struggle against the forces of darkness.

How much time do you spend each day praying? Someone once said that a prayerless Christian is a powerless Christian— and that person was right! You need to take more time to pray each day besides just the quick few words you say before a meal. "Rubba dub dub, here comes the grub, bless this food" isn't going to do much good in our struggle against evil.

The armor of God is not optional for Christians. It is essential for victory against the forces of darkness. Each piece was carefully designed by God to serve a specific purpose. When properly "put on" and utilized, God's armor enables us to withstand the devil's evil schemes and attacks.

Because Satan never exercises a cease-fire in the battle, we must always be on the alert for attack. That's why it is crucial to put on the full armor of God every day. Take a few minutes briefly each morning to pray about each piece and carefully put it in place in your life.

God has done an awesome job of providing all the necessary equipment to stand up to the enemy forces in battle. Now it's up to us to secure the equipment, get trained in how to use it, and, most important, use it!

Think about it

1. What are you trusting God for today that only He can accomplish? Be specific and take time to prayerfully consider this.

2. Read Proverbs 30:5 NIV carefully. What does it mean to "take refuge" in God? How can you do this?

3. What three pieces of "battle gear" in Ephesians 6:16–17 must we take up? Why are these pieces of "gear" so important in standing up to the devil?

4. Read Philippians 4:6–7. What must we do to experience God's peace in the midst of attacks from the Enemy?

CHAPTER 14

CHOOSE YOUR WEAPONS

You're a soldier in a spiritual war. This is not an optional situation for anyone. Like it or not, you're fighting in an intensive, unseen battle. But you do have a couple of choices to make regarding how you function in combat. First, you must decide who your commanding officer is: the devil or Jesus. Who is it that you take your orders from? If you have never put your faith and trust in Jesus as Savior and Lord, I want you to jump ahead to the next chapter, "Freedom From the Power of Darkness," and seriously consider this commitment. Then, once you've taken care of establishing a relationship with Christ, return to this chapter.

Second, you must choose your weapons. Will you fight the battle with human weapons or with God-given spiritual weapons? The Enemy is defeating many Christians today because they're trying to use human weapons in a supernatural battle.

Every Christian has been given the equipment essential for victory in the daily struggle against the world, our sinful nature, and the devil. The two most crucial weapons are the Sword of the Spirit (the Bible) and prayer. Let's take a look at the Sword first and see how we can best utilize this weapon.

THE SWORD

The Holy Spirit is our resident teacher of truth. He makes the Bible effective in our lives. In the previous chapter I mentioned that a Roman soldier's sword is usually a small, easily handled dagger, used for up-close precision work. The Word of God must also be handled specifically and precisely to be effective in a believer's life.

The problem is that too many teens today are not using their swords, and there seems to be confusion about what the Bible actually teaches, what they believe, and how it affects their lives. Consider the findings of a recent study among Christian teens:

+ Only 36 percent say they read the Bible outside of church during the week.
+ Only 28 percent participate in a small group—not including Sunday school—for Bible study, prayer, and fellowship during the week.
+ 60 percent say the Bible is totally accurate in all of its teachings.
+ 75 percent believe that all the miracles described in the Bible actually took place.
+ 75 percent suggest that the Bible provides us with practical standards for contemporary life.
+ 75 percent believe that a central message of the Bible is that God helps those who help themselves.
+ Nearly 60 percent believe that all religious faiths teach equally valid truths.[1]

No wonder so many teens are leading defeated Christian lives. One of the most important weapons we have is hardly being used, and when it is, there seems to be a lot of confusion about what the Bible actually teaches.

Before we look at specific ways to study and use "the sword," let's take time to answer some common questions about this awesome weapon.

HOW IS THE BIBLE DIFFERENT?

The Bible is the written Word of God. The Bible was written over a fifteen-hundred-year span of time by forty-four different authors—all living in different places—in three languages: Hebrew, Aramaic, and Greek. It's an amazing book for its unity in the midst of vast diversity. Think about it. The Bible has one continuous drama from Genesis to Revelation—the rescue of humanity. It has a central theme—the person of Jesus Christ. And from the beginning to the end, the Bible has one unified message—humanity's problem is sin, and the remedy is found in Jesus. All this evidence points to the fact that one mind is behind the writing of the Bible.

The uniqueness of the Bible's message is summed up in Romans 6:23: "The wages of sin is death, but the free gift of God is eternal life through Christ Jesus our Lord." Christianity teaches that all people are spiritually dead and there is no hope that we can fix ourselves. Other religions say just the opposite. They agree there is something wrong spiritually, but they hold out hope that somehow, through our own human effort, we can be fixed. The Bible makes it clear that spiritually dead people can't fix themselves (Ephesians 2:8–9). And because God is holy, He cannot have a relationship with sinful people. The problem is that we all have sinned (Romans 3:23).

But even though we have this horrible spiritual condition, there is good news: God has a remedy. He demonstrated His love for us by sacrificing Jesus on the cross to pay the penalty for our sin (Romans 5:8). Because of Jesus' death and resurrection, we can be forgiven for our sin and have a new power for living. We can also have eternal life—not just some continued existence on another spiritual plane after death. We can actually have fellowship with God himself (John 17:3). No other religion in the world promises eternal life and closeness with the living God (Hebrews 4:16). And it starts in this life—the moment we place our faith and trust in Jesus Christ. Finally, this message is unique because eternal life is a free gift. It's not a gift that can be earned; it can only be received. We can have this gift by admitting our need for life because of our spiritual death rather than relying on the work Jesus did for us by paying the penalty for our sin (Ephesians 2:8–9).

CAN YOU TRUST THE BIBLE?

People today are searching for real answers they can trust, something to help them sort through the confusion. They're looking for a source of authority they can rely on. The Word of God is the only source we can trust for answers about the issues of life.

There's not enough room in a book like this to discuss every reason we can trust the Bible, but here are a few things to think about.

The Bible is unique in its ability to have survived over the course of time, through criticism and persecution. It actually has more ancient manuscript evidence to support it than any ten pieces of classical literature combined. Throughout history people have tried to burn and outlaw the Bible. Others have spent their life trying to refute it—even so-called scholars. Yet the Bible has endured all its enemies and has been able to stand up to even the most persistent critics.

When tested by the same criteria that other historical manuscripts are tested, the Bible demonstrates incredible accuracy for the historical events it reports. For example, did you know there are 5,656 partial and complete manuscript portions (in Greek) of the New Testament alone? In comparison, the next closest historical manuscript is Homer's *Iliad* with only 643 copies. Then we need to consider supporting evidence that comes from sources such as early Christian writers outside the Bible, like Clement of Rome, Ignatius, and Polycarp. And consider support from non-Christian historical writers such as Tacitus and Josephus.

And then we need to examine archaeological evidence that supports the Bible. The Bible is unique because it's the only book in the world to offer specific predictions about the future, written hundreds of years in advance, that were literally fulfilled. A lot of these predictions focus on the first and second comings of Christ. There are several unique things about prophecies in the Bible in contrast to other attempts made to predict future events. These unique features include:

+ The prophecies are very specific.
+ None of these predictions ever failed.
+ Since the prophecies about Christ were written hundreds of years before His birth, no one could have even been making intelligent guesses.
+ The fulfillment of many of these predictions was beyond human ability to force.

And what about the Bible's unique impact on civilization, as well as on literature? We must also recognize the Bible's unique teachings on character and history. It's amazing when you consider all the events throughout history that were predicted in the Bible hundreds, sometimes even thousands, of years in advance. No unconditional prophecy of the Bible about events to the present day has gone unfilled. Other books, such as the Koran, the Book of Mormon, and parts of the (Hindu) Veda, claim divine inspiration. But none of those books contains predictive prophecy that is completely accurate. Fulfilled prophecy is another sign of the unique divine authority of the Bible.

The Bible is our ultimate source of truth. It doesn't make sense why anyone would want to base his or her eternal destiny—and life on the planet—on someone's opinion when we have God's Word available to help us and guide us. The core message of the Bible, which sets it apart from every other book in all of history, is the offer of the free gift of eternal life through Jesus Christ.

There's no doubt the Bible deserves our careful attention.

WHY SHOULD I STUDY THE BIBLE?

We live in a "what's in it for me?" society. People want to know how they're going to benefit from being involved in certain activities. This kind of thinking has transferred into the spiritual dimension of life, especially when it comes to spending time studying the Bible.

The benefits of regular study of God's Word far outweigh any sacrifice of time and energy on our part. Four of the main advantages are found in 2 Timothy 3:16–17:

> All Scripture is inspired by God and is useful to teach us what is true and to make us realize what is wrong in our lives. It corrects us when we are wrong and teaches us to do what is right. God uses it to prepare and equip his people to do every good work.

Everything in the Bible is beneficial and deserves our attention. When we read God's Word, He is speaking directly to us. Let's look more carefully at the four main advantages mentioned in these two verses.

Teaches us. The Bible helps to shape our thinking God's way.

We need to think correctly so we can live correctly. Someone once said that what you believe is how you will behave. The Bible gives us all the divine truth we need for living a meaningful, godly life.

Helps us realize what's wrong in our lives. God tells us through His Word when we're out-of-bounds in our life—wrong in our behavior or in our beliefs. The Holy Spirit convicts us of the things that need to be changed. The Bible not only tells us what is sin but also what God desires in our life.

Corrects us. The Bible helps us to correct the problem by pointing the way back to God's pathway. It opens up the doors in our life and enables us to clean out the sin. The Bible helps us to straighten things up and put them back in proper order.

Helps us to do what is right. The Bible shows us how to live the way we were created to live. It's our handbook for living filled with positive guidelines on how to get the most out of life. It's the greatest owner's manual ever written, answering the questions we have and guiding us in the decisions we make.

The bottom line is that the Bible helps us to grow in our relationship with God and teaches us how to get the most out of life—to live the way we were created to live.

But if the Bible is so unique, trustworthy, and valuable, why don't people spend more time reading it?

We could come up with a bunch of excuses. Maybe it's because we have become so visually oriented with TV, DVDs, and computers that the Bible doesn't appeal to us as much. Or because we don't think we have the time. Or the Bible doesn't seem relevant. It's easy to come up with a zillion and one bad excuses why we don't spend time in God's Word. Take a minute and check out your own habits:

+ How often do you read the Bible?

+ When you do read it, how much time do you spend?
+ Do you do what it says?
+ If you don't read it, why not? (Think very specifically.)

I'm convinced the devil will throw any number of obstacles in our way to keep us out of the Bible. Some will even be things that are good in themselves. That's all the more reason to make Bible study a priority and discipline ourselves to make time for it on a consistent basis. Satan recognizes the power of Scripture, and so should we. Studying God's Word provides the ultimate protection for daily battles against the Enemy, the world, and our sinful nature.

Before we get into some real, practical, hands-on ways to get into the Word, let's take a quick look at another crucial piece of "battle gear" we'll need if we're going to experience victory in the daily struggles with enemy forces.

PRAYER

Someone once said that Satan trembles when he sees the weakest Christian on his or her knees. As we discussed in the last chapter, there is no doubt that prayer is the most important piece of equipment we have for spiritual warfare. Prayer is more than expressing our thoughts to God or presenting our list of wants and needs to Him. Prayer demonstrates our total dependence on the Lord for His help, hope, and guidance.

People from all walks of life have come to realize the value and necessity of prayer. President Abraham Lincoln once said, "I have been driven many times to my knees by the overwhelming conviction that I had nowhere else to go. My own wisdom, and that of all about me, seemed insufficient for the day."

Have you reached that place in your life where you realize prayer is not the only place you can go but also the best place you can turn to for help? Prayer for the Christian is like spiritual breathing—an absolute necessity for life!

Prayer is probably the most misunderstood and underused part of the Christian life. It's much more than some meaningless repetition we sometimes get caught up in to fulfill our "spiritual duty." We often fail to realize the significance, power, and privilege of prayer. Imagine the Creator of the universe actually listening to us and responding to our needs. It's awesome!

Like anything else associated with spiritual growth, we must dedicate quality time to prayer. There's a price to pay, but what we stand to gain far outweighs any cost involved. Whatever you have to do with school, relationships, sports, or a job—nothing is more important than developing your spiritual life; it affects everything else.

In the rest of this chapter we will look at some practical tips on how to develop a consistent time alone with God.

GETTING INTO THE WORD AND PRAYER

This section on the practical how-to's is not meant to make you feel guilty or overwhelm you with totally unrealistic expectations for spending time in the Bible and prayer. If you're already spending time alone with God, I hope this section will be an encouragement to you to keep doing what you're doing and maybe give you some tips on how to improve and strengthen your Bible study and prayer time.

If this is something you'd like to start doing, I want to help you understand how you can study the Bible for yourself and start developing your prayer life. We'll work at setting some practical, obtainable goals so you can gradually develop the habit of a daily, consistent time alone with God. But let's be realistic. If you're not doing it now, you can't expect to go from nothing to everything overnight. After all, how do you eat an elephant? One bite at a time! How do you develop a consistent time alone with God? One day at a time!

Before you actually start having a regular time alone with God, here are some things to think about.

1. Set a consistent time and place. Make an appointment with God and keep it. Don't let anything keep you from that time. I think morning usually works the best. Time alone with God early helps us to prepare to face the challenges of the day. Make sure the place you have chosen will be free from distractions, and remember to turn off the TV, computer, and your iPod. Try to get rid of all the things that might distract you.

2. Set realistic goals for yourself about how often and how much you will read. For example, you could start by planning to spend time alone with God three days this week. If you end up doing more, great! But it's better to start slow and gradually increase it rather than to crash and burn the first week.

Start by planning to spend about fifteen minutes each day with Him. If you want to spend more time, awesome! The important thing is to be realistic and work at developing consistency.

3. Have a plan for reading and studying. There are several ways you can develop a plan for studying the Bible, depending on what you'd like to do. You can choose to read through a book in the Old or New Testament. For example, you could decide to read a chapter in Proverbs every day or in one of the gospels (Matthew, Mark, Luke, or John). A chapter is always a good way to start, but the issue isn't how much you read, but how to make sure you understand what you've read and apply it to your daily life.

You could do a word study on a subject that interests you. Most Bibles have a concordance in the back, and with that you can look up words like *love, peace, anger,* or whatever you choose. Take notes about what the Bible has to say about that word and how it's used.

A topical study is another way to spend your time in God's Word. The best resource for this is a topical Bible that lists various subjects and where they can be found in the Bible.

You can also do a character study of a particular person in the Bible. There are some fascinating people in God's Word who can teach us a lot about life. At the end of this chapter there are some ideas to help you get started in all these different kinds of studies.

If you're not a big reader or have trouble reading, think about getting a copy of the Bible on CD or find a podcast online. It's a great way to study the Bible as you spend time alone with God. It also has the advantage of helping you grow as you jog, work out, or drive. Most Christian bookstores have several different versions on CD, or you can look online.

4. Have a plan for taking notes on what you learn from studying God's Word. As you read the Bible, keep certain questions in mind about the passage:

+ What's happening? What is the outcome? What is God's promise for me?
+ Who is talking or being talked about? (Principal characters)
+ Where did this take place? Where have they been? Where are they going?
+ When did this happen? (In history or the life of this person)
+ Why did this happen? Why was it important to be said?
+ How does this apply to me? What do I need to do?

Take time to carefully examine the verses you read in light

of these questions. Don't be afraid to underline key verses or circle key words that grab your attention. If you have a question, make a note about it and ask your youth pastor, a parent, or a friend.

KEEPING TRACK OF WHAT YOU DISCOVER

Once you decide on your plan, you'll find it helpful to have a place to take notes on what you are discovering. Take some time to develop a spiritual journal to keep track of what you are reading, learning, and praying about.

Check out your local Christian bookstore or an online store for a variety of journals. There are also some sample forms at the end of this chapter if you want to put your own journal together. (Feel free to photocopy the forms for your own use.) Following those study forms, you'll find some ideas for word studies, books, topics, and characters. It's not an exhaustive list, but it will get you started.

The reason we study the Bible and spend time praying is that we want to grow in our relationship with God. Spending time alone with the Lord helps us to know Him better and to become more like Jesus in the way we think and live.

THINK ABOUT IT

1. What is the best time of day for you to spend time alone with God? Make an appointment with Him by setting a specific time now. (Start with morning, afternoon, or nighttime.)
2. Where would be the best place in your house to be alone with God? Make sure that you will not be disturbed by a pet, family member, the TV, etc.
3. What's your starting goal for the number of days you will

spend time in Bible study and prayer during the next week? Be realistic and be specific.

4. What type of plan are you going to follow for studying the Bible? Be sure to start with something that interests you. It'll help you to stay motivated.

5. What's the biggest challenge or concern you are facing right now? Spend the next few minutes in prayer, asking for God's direction and help for the situation. Make sure you list this prayer request in your journal or on the prayer form at the end of this chapter.

FORMS

Bible study

Date: _____

1. Verse(s) reference: _____

2. Main theme or thought (one sentence):

_____

_____

_____

3. Key word or verse:

_____

_____

_____

4. Summary (Write a short paragraph summarizing what the author is saying.):

_____

_____

_____

5. What does it say to me? (How can I apply this truth to my life?):

_____

_____

_____

6. Action (What do I need to do? When, where, and with whom?):

_____

_____

_____

7. God's promise (where appropriate):

_____

_____

_____

Prayer requests

What am I asking God to do, answer, or provide?	Date requested	Date answered

Friends and family who need Jesus	Date accepted Christ

Study Ideas to Help Get You Started

Word studies

+ *Love:* Matthew 5:43, 22:37; John 15:13; 1 Corinthians 13; Ephesians 2:4–5
+ *Evil:* Genesis 2:9; Judges 3:7; Job 1:8; Psalm 34:14; Proverbs 8:13
+ *Trust:* Psalm 9:10, 13:5; Isaiah 26:4; John 14:1; Hebrews 2:13
+ *Hope:* Psalm 25:5, 42:5; Proverbs 23:18; Jeremiah 29:11; Philippians 2:19
+ *Peace:* Psalm 34:14; Proverbs 14:30; Isaiah 9:6; Romans 5:1; Philippians 4:7

Book studies

+ Psalms
+ Proverbs
+ Ecclesiastes
+ Mark
+ Ephesians
+ James

Topical studies

+ *Loneliness:* 1 Kings 18 and 19
+ *Growth and maturity:* Romans 5:1–11, 6:1–14
+ *Assurance:* Ephesians 1:7; Romans 8:38–39; 1 John 5:13; Philippians 1:6
+ *Lordship:* 1 Corinthians 6:19–20; Matthew 22:37–38; Psalm 37:4–5; Luke 6:46
+ *Prayer:* John 16:24; Matthew 7:7; Jeremiah 33:3; Ephesians 3:20; James 1:5

+ *Telling others about Jesus:* Matthew 4:19, 5:16; 1 Peter 3:15; Acts 1:8, 4:20, 16:31; 2 Corinthians 5:20
+ *The Holy Spirit:* Ephesians 5:18; 2 Timothy 1:7; Galatians 5:22–26
+ *Obedience:* Ecclesiastes 12:13; Deuteronomy 6:5–6; John 14:21

Character studies

+ *Ruth:* Book of Ruth
+ *Job:* Book of Job
+ *Jonah:* Book of Jonah

CHAPTER 15

FREEDOM FROM THE POWER OF DARKNESS

Dear Steve,

Howz it goin? I heard you speak last month, and I just wanted to thank you. I had been involved in the occult for over a year. I was a third-rank leader, and I helped lead some of the rituals that we went through.

Last year I "rededicated" my life to Christ, but only as a joke. I felt that if God really loved me more than Satan, He would have given me the life I wanted. Our group used to go through many satanic rituals and other things to worship the devil. We'd do anything for Satan.

After listening to you speak, I realized that God was real and Satan wasn't the person I should be worshiping. I accepted Christ at your meeting, and I'm glad I did. When I returned home, I found out that the police had picked up one of the guys under my leadership. He'd mentioned my name along with many other names of the people in our group. He's now being tried for vandalism and murder.

God used this situation to allow me to drop out of the occult in order to stay out of juvenile hall. I realize now that I'd been missing out on God's love because I had turned to Satan out of bitterness. I'm now trying to spread God's love instead of Satan's lies. My story may not seem to be the greatest testimony, but I feel that if God can help me to get out of the occult, then maybe my story can help others realize that God is more powerful than Satan, and He can help anybody out of any situation. I've also learned that no matter what you've done, God will forgive you and help you to receive His love and eternal life.

Love always,
Tiffany

As Tiffany found out, there is hope, help, and power to be found in the person of Jesus Christ. Satan is cruel, clever, and destructive. His power goes way beyond our human abilities. If you're not plugged in to the power of God, if you don't have a relationship with Jesus, then you can't hope to be able to resist the devil and the power of evil around you.

Hanging around a church doesn't make you a Christian or give you some kind of special power. Some students live a totally worldly life all week long and then show up at the youth group meeting on Sunday or Wednesday and play the game. They are like chameleons—they change with their surroundings. Have you checked out your motives? Are you really committed to God? Do you really know Jesus?

CHOOSING TO FOLLOW JESUS

The most important thing you can do in life is to make a sincere commitment to live your life for and like Jesus. To follow Jesus Christ as your Savior and Lord. Then it's up to you to make an effort to grow in this very special relationship with the living God. Jesus is standing before you today with His arms open wide, saying, "Trust me. Believe in me. I love you and want to have an intimate relationship with you." Jesus is not only our defender, He's also our Savior. Jesus died on a cross to make a new and exciting life possible for us.

The dark occult world of Satan may have a certain appeal—temporarily—but the God of the Bible has a zillion times more to offer in a personal relationship with Him. But we must *choose* to follow and obey Jesus. No one can make this decision for you, and going to church, listening to praise music, or even being a good person isn't enough. You must totally surrender your life to Jesus—give Him control.

If you have not yet decided to put your faith and trust in Jesus, I want to give you an opportunity to do it now. Freedom from the power of darkness begins when you surrender your life to Christ. It's the truth that sets you free. Jesus said in John 14:6, "I am the way, the truth, and the life. No one can come to the Father except through me."

But keep in mind that this decision will cost you. It will cost you your favorite sins and your self-centered attitude to try to live your life without God. It may cost you some friends who don't understand why your life is so different. The decision to follow Jesus may even cost you your dreams about the future, because God may have something planned for you that you never expected—much better than you could ever imagine. The cost is high to become a follower of Christ, but it is not anywhere near what it will cost you to ignore God and try to live without Him.

If you're ready to start a relationship with Jesus Christ, take a few minutes right now and follow the simple steps listed below. It's an easy way to establish a relationship with the living God. Deciding to live your life for and like Jesus is the most important decision you will ever make. There's nothing greater than experiencing God's love, forgiveness, and acceptance. Once you've made the decision to follow Jesus, life takes on a whole new meaning.

It's not complicated and you can do it right now. Check out this promise from God's Word in Romans 10:9: "If you confess with your mouth that Jesus is Lord and believe in your heart that God raised him from the dead, you will be saved."

Here's how you can start a relationship with Jesus:

1. Admit that you are a sinner.
2. Be willing to turn away from your sins (repent).

3. Believe that Jesus died for you on the cross and rose from the grave.
4. Through prayer, surrender your life to Jesus and ask Him to be in charge of your life through the Holy Spirit.

You can pray something like this:

Dear Jesus,

I know that I have sinned and need your forgiveness. I want to turn away from my sins to live my life for you and like you. I believe that you died on the cross to pay the penalty for my sins and that you came back to life after three days. I surrender my heart and my life to you. I ask you to save me from the punishment of my sins, and I want to follow you as the boss of my life. Thank you for your love and for your gift of eternal life.

In Jesus' name. Amen.

Did you decide to surrender your life to Jesus? If so, you've made the most important decision of your life! If you have sincerely accepted Christ, then you can trust Him. Check out what the Bible says in Romans 10:13: "Anyone who calls on the name of the Lord will be saved."

When we surrender our lives to Jesus, we become brand-new people. Check out the promise in 2 Corinthians 5:17: "What this means is that those who become Christians become new persons. They are not the same anymore, for the old life is gone. A new life has begun!"

We may still look the same on the outside, but God makes us totally new people on the inside. You don't just change some stuff in your life, you start a new one—this time with a new Master. God supernaturally changes us the minute we surrender our lives to Jesus. We now can have a close relationship with Him because sin no longer separates us. That's why it's important now to take time each day to grow even closer in our relationship with God. We can do this by studying the Bible and talking with God in prayer.

Becoming a Christian is not just something you add to your life—it's something that becomes your life. You look the same on the outside, but you're a totally different person on the inside. You've been given an awesome new power to help you with the tough stuff in life. The power you now have available to you is the same power that brought Jesus back to life from the grave on the very first Easter Sunday. It's called resurrection power, and it's available to help with all the difficult issues and pain in your life. This power never runs out, and you can only get it from the living God of the Bible. This is something no other religion can offer. But there's a catch—in order to get this new life, you have to surrender the old one. You must give up control and decide to live your life for Jesus—not for yourself.

When it comes to Jesus and the kingdom of God, things are just the opposite. Jesus told His followers in Matthew 16:25, "If you try to hang on to your life, you will lose it. But if you give up your life for my sake, you will save it." Surrendering your life to someone else is always hard because you no longer maintain control. But you are not just surrendering to anyone—it's the Creator God, the One who made you and knows what is best for you. The only way we can experience real purpose in our life, as well as wisdom for the tough stuff we face, is by surrendering our lives to Jesus.

This relationship that you have established is one that cannot be broken or terminated—even in death. Jesus promises to never let you down and never give you up (Hebrews 13:5). This is the heart of Christianity. It's not a just religion: it's God revealing himself to us, rescuing us from our sin and making it possible for us to experience a relationship with Him.

You may feel totally different right now, or you may not. The most important thing is that you have started this relationship with the living God, and you have the rest of eternity to develop and experience it!

And, by the way, if you did decide to live your life for and like Jesus, please let me know by using the contact information in the back of this book. This is just the beginning of a great new life with Jesus. I want to pray for you and send you stuff—including a CD—to help you get started growing in your new relationship with God.

You're already a Christian, but . . .

What do you do when you've already put your faith and trust in Jesus and still don't seem to be experiencing freedom? You try and try and try, but your Christian life just isn't working. It's possible that somehow the Enemy has gained a foothold in your life (Ephesians 4:27). Your eternal relationship with God isn't at stake, but you need to take responsibility for taking a stand against the Enemy's lies. You must choose truth in the battle for your mind and emotions. The devil works subtly to gain a foothold in your life through things like unforgiveness, bitterness, jealousy, and even pornography. That's why it is so important to let the Bible work as a filter for what you read, watch, and listen to. And as we read and study it, we need to be careful to do what it says—obey God—when it relates to things like unforgiveness, bitterness, jealousy, and any other area where Satan may have established a foothold.

Spend some time in prayer and ask God to show you any areas of your life where the devil may have gained a foothold. Ask God for wisdom in dealing with these issues so you will not be influenced by Satan in them.

NOW WHAT?

We've covered a lot of important information in this chapter. Remember, continue to be aware of the devil's attempts to try to gain a foothold. He is relentless in his schemes to influence your thinking. The spiritual war will never be over until we go to be with Jesus or until He returns.

Our freedom in Christ is eternally secure, but it needs to be maintained on a daily basis. This means that you must keep up your relationship with Jesus. If you find yourself slipping or falling in your spiritual life, get back to the basics. Keep short accounts with God in relation to your sin, and make sure you're spending consistent quality time in the Bible and prayer. Stay involved in your church youth group and double-check to make sure that you have your "battle gear" on.

Jesus has the power and authority to boot the enemy and his forces of darkness out of our lives. But it's our responsibility not to open the door and let the devil back in.

The Lord has promised to never leave us or abandon us (Hebrews 13:5). So stand up to the devil, don't dabble in the darkness, and keep your eyes on Jesus!

THINK ABOUT IT

1. What does the phrase "freedom from the power of darkness" mean to you?
2. What areas of your life are vulnerable to the devil gaining a foothold? What can you do—with God's help—to avoid this happening?
3. Why is it so important to maintain the spiritual basics in your life? (Bible study, prayer, etc.)

CHAPTER 16

CANDLE IN THE DARK

Brandi came to me out of concern for a friend. She explained how one of her girl friends seemed to be totally consumed by the occult and Satan worship. "She doesn't see the danger or even how much her involvement in this darkness is changing her," Brandi said. "I want to help her so badly, but I don't know what to do. Where do I start?"

What can we do to help those we care about come out of the darkness and into the light?

God has given us an awesome privilege to be soldiers, under His command, deployed in a massive hostage-rescue operation. He has made us light so we might bring others to Jesus (Acts 13:47).

All around us are friends, family members, neighbors, and people at school who are living in darkness. The devil has done a masterful job at getting them to believe his lies and taking them hostage (2 Timothy 2:26). They have no sense of purpose or direction because they've never made a decision to follow Jesus.

And just like Brandi's friend, some people we care about are actually playing with fire and don't recognize the danger of their dabbling in the darkness. How can we recognize if a friend is playing in the devil's playground? Here are some warning signs to look for:

1. *Withdrawal from routine activities—the normal everyday stuff*
   Beware of unusual seclusion and secrecy by your friend.

2. *Obsession with death and suicide.* Pay attention to the music your friend is listening to and the DVDs he or she is watching (and anything else that's feeding his or her mind), especially those that may have occult themes. Also check any doodles or scribbles on a notebook or book cover with these themes.

3. *Obsession with black.* Your friend could demonstrate this obsession by dyeing his or her hair black, wearing dark makeup to an extreme, or dressing totally in black all the time. But be careful not to overreact, because black is also simply a fashionable color.

4. *Fixation with satanic/occult symbols.* These symbols can be found on a variety of items, including jewelry, clothing, CD covers, comic books, games, etc. Many of these symbols are explained in appendix A of this book.

5. *Possession of "how to" satanic or Wiccan literature.* These could include a copy of the *Satanic Bible,* books like *Magick* by Aleister Crowley, manuals on how to cast spells, etc.

6. *Excessive fears or anxiety.* If your friend exhibits unusual preoccupation and paranoia about current events in the world, at school, or at home, then you have a reason to be concerned.

7. *Fascination with or possession of knives.* Ceremonial knives of various sizes and shapes are used in satanic rituals, black masses, and sacrifices. It's usually pretty obvious if your friend's interest is more than just an innocent collection.

8. *Cuts, scratches, burns, and tattoos.* Look for scars or tattoos in the shape of satanic or occult symbols on various parts of the body.

9. *Books and journals.* Watch for a Book of Shadows, drawings, poetry, or books that focus on death, the occult, Satan worship, black magic, reincarnation, or witchcraft. Anything written in blood, backward script, a homemade alphabet, or a secret code could be connected to the occult.

10. *Satanic altars.* These can be simple or extremely elaborate and located in a bedroom closet, basement, garage, or attic. Very often red, black, or white candles illuminate them. They can be decorated with ritual knives and even animal bones.

To rescue someone from this minefield, we must first fully understand the level of commitment and preparation that needs to be in place in our own lives. Like all good soldiers, we must prepare for battle. In chapter 13 we learned about the "battle gear" God has provided for us. Now let's look at how we can practically use these weapons to make a difference in our world.

HOW TO BE GOD'S CANDLE

If you want to be used by God as a "candle" in your home, at work, in the neighborhood, or on your campus, take time to evaluate your own life in comparison to each of these "how to" steps.

Stay close to Jesus

We're secure in Christ, and we belong to Him. There's nothing we can do to help others or ourselves in the spiritual battle apart from Jesus. He is our protection, our strength, our defender, and our greatest resource as we face the powers of darkness.

The devil will attempt to make you think you can fight the spiritual battle in your own strength, but keep your heart and mind centered on God's Word. Continue to develop an intimate relationship with the Lord Jesus as you spend time in prayer and the Bible. His absolute truth will give you the ability to withstand the deceptive attacks of the Enemy.

Be careful of the "demon-buster complex." God has

called us to kick the devil in the bum. Nor has He called us to go on some sort of search-and-destroy mission to flush out the Enemy. Numerous times in the Bible the Lord reminds us to stand firm against the devil and he will flee from us. It *doesn't* tell us to attack him; don't go gunning for trouble. Instead, when the attack comes, rely on the strength of the Lord. He will give you victory. Stay as close to Jesus as you possibly can on a daily basis. This is one area of your life you don't want to slack off in.

Don't be afraid

Beware of Satan's use of fear to sidetrack you from being a godly influence in your world. A well-meaning missionary called while I was writing another book on spiritual warfare to warn me about completing the project. A drunk driver had just killed two members of our team in a tragic car accident. This missionary said my two friends died because I was writing a book about the devil. "You'd better quit working on this book before the devil kills you too," he said. "Call the publisher and tell them you want out immediately."

Had I followed his advice, I would have given in to the devil's fear tactic—and that has no place in my life as a Christian. If we run in the face of the Enemy's attacks, we are denying the power of the living God. Satan's power is limited; God's power is unlimited. We must find a balance between attributing to Satan more power than he has and not respecting the power he actually does have. While we are facing a fierce opponent, the Bible reminds us that God is greater and will keep us from all evil if we trust Him.

Check and recheck your battle gear

No soldier in his right mind would go off to war without the ᴇr equipment. As Christian soldiers in a spiritual battle, we are no different. The "battle gear" God has given us is absolutely critical. Make it a practice each day to check and recheck your "equipment." Make sure that to the best of your knowledge, everything is securely in place. You can do this through prayer. Open up your Bible to Ephesians 6:13–18, and then pray something like this:

Dear Lord,
   By faith I want to stand up to the devil by putting on the belt of truth today. Help me to resist the attacks of Satan. Thank you for providing spiritual armor for my protection.
   I pray this in the powerful name of Jesus. Amen.

Pray this simple prayer for each piece of equipment listed in those verses every day.

Pray

Finally, the most important thing you or I can do in attempting to rescue friends or a relative from the darkness is to pray for them. Our first strategic step should be on our knees, asking God through His might and power to break the chains of darkness that hold them prisoner.

Remember, our first objective in rescuing spiritual hostages is to influence then to live their lives for and like Jesus. If our friends or relatives don't have a personal relationship with Jesus, no matter what we might try to do, they will still be a prisoner of the enemy. If you're not sure how to share Christ with someone, look back at the last chapter for some tips. Then, once you're sure of the person's relationship with Jesus, you can help him or her pray through any stubborn habits or sin. When you're leading someone to Christ or helping them pray through sinful habits, make sure you recruit others to pray for you.

We are involved in a battle for truth, not power. We must help our friends and family accept God's truth and stop believing the lies that Satan has fed their minds. Satan's only power is in his deceptive lies. The light of God's truth shatters the lies of the devil and sets us free to be the people God designed us to be.

There's no greater privilege than to be used by God to rescue others from the darkness, making a difference that will count for all eternity.

BE A CANDLE IN YOUR WORLD

Do you want to make your life really count? Are you tired of being bored and looking for some meaning in your life—a reason to get up in the morning?

Then ask God to use you as a candle in the darkness of your home, neighborhood, campus, and world. No matter how old you are or what weaknesses you may have, don't let anyone put you down or make you feel incapable of being used by God. Instead, remember what the Bible says in 1 Timothy 4:12: "Don't let anyone think less of you because you are young. Be an example to all believers in what you say, in the way you live, in your love, your faith, and your purity."

I owe my life to someone just like you, and that's why I'm so committed to helping students be all that God designed them to be. Robbie was taking drum lessons from me while I was in the music industry. Each week during his lesson he would tell me about his best friend. Rob told me how he shared everything with this friend, but he never told me his best friend's name. I actually started to become jealous of Robbie and his best friend's relationship because I didn't have a friend like that. One day I finally asked Robbie what his best friend's name was, and his response just about knocked me over. "Jesus," Robbie said.

"And He can be your best friend too." A short time later, I met Robbie's aunt and uncle, Billy and Danielle, who were also in the music industry and strong Christians, and they led me to Christ.

As a result of one student's courage to tell me that I needed Jesus, people across the United States, Canada, and in twenty-five foreign countries have heard me communicate the message of God's love.

✝ ✝ ✝

Jim came to me out of concern for a friend who was deeply involved in Wicca and messing around with spells and sorcery. "Steve, I know what my friend is doing is dangerous spiritually, but I don't quite know how to explain it to him," he said. I was able to give Jim some CDs and booklets that helped him to point out the dangers of dabbling with the darkness. Now his friend is coming to youth group and is involved with more positive things to challenge his creative mind.

✝ ✝ ✝

Lori and a couple of her friends became very concerned when they learned that almost two hundred kids on their campus had been referred to professional counseling during the first six weeks of school because of their involvement in the occult. They decided to meet once a week after school to pray for the issues plaguing students on their campus and to discuss the Bible together. Before long there were forty to fifty students and a Christian teacher meeting together once a week to pray and study the Bible. The problem of students involved with the occult hasn't disappeared, but it's gotten a lot better. With all that's happened, Lori and her friends are constantly looking for more ways to be candles on their campus.

†††

David plays on the water polo team at his high school. One day at practice, a couple of his teammates got into a fight, and the coach pulled them out to the sidelines. David remembered what his youth pastor had been discussing at the last youth group meeting: "As iron sharpens iron, so a friend sharpens a friend" (Proverbs 27:17). He shared that verse with his teammates and told them how much more effective they would be if they worked together instead of fighting. Since that time, David has had several opportunities to share more practical principles from the Bible with other people on his campus.

†††

God used these students. He wants to use you too. As you become aware of different issues troubling those around you, ask God how He wants to use you to be that candle of light in a dark world. Jesus said in Matthew 5:14–16, "You are the light of the world—like a city on a hilltop that cannot be hidden. No one lights a lamp and then puts it under a basket. Instead, a lamp is placed on a stand, where it gives light to everyone in the house. In the same way, let your good deeds shine out for all to see, so that everyone will praise your heavenly Father."

ONE PERSON CAN MAKE A DIFFERENCE

In Romania in December 1989, Communist authorities sent police to arrest Laszlo Tokes, the pastor of the Hungarian

Reformed Church in the town of Timisoara. But when they arrived, the police found a solid wall of people blocking the entrance to the church. Members of many different churches had joined together in protest. The people didn't budge for the police. They held their ground the entire day and into the night. Shortly after midnight, a nineteen-year-old student named Daniel Gavra pulled out a packet of candles. Lighting one, he passed it to the person next to him.

Then he lit another candle and another one after that. One by one the brightly shining candles were passed out among the crowd. Very soon the light of hundreds of candles pierced the darkness of that cold December night. Christians came together in unity, disregarding denominational differences and joining hands in the pastor's defense. Even though the crowd stayed through the night and the next day, the police finally broke through and arrested the pastor and his family.

But that was not the end. The religious protest led to political protest in the city as people moved to the town square to begin a full-scale demonstration against the Communist government. Once again, Daniel passed out candles. Ultimately, troops were brought in to squelch the demonstration. Hundreds were shot, and Daniel's leg was blown off. But despite the opposition, their example inspired the whole nation of Romania and ultimately caused the collapse of the evil dictator Nicolae Ceausescu.[1]

One teenage guy lit the candle that eventually lit up a whole country! It takes only a small flame in a dark world to make a difference. Will you be the first candle in the darkness in your home, on your campus, on your job, in your community?

FINAL THOUGHTS

We've covered a lot of important things in this book. Now you know what you're up against in the spiritual battle. And even though we have an enemy who is bent on our destruction, we can have victory in the spiritual conflict in which we are engaged.

The devil will try any way possible to influence our thinking. The spiritual battle will ultimately be won or lost in the mind. That's why it's so important to stay alert mentally to the temptations that may come our way through music, games, Web sites, movies and TV shows, witchcraft, New Age philosophies, and a number of other things. As the battle rages for your mind, take control and make sure you're adequately prepared.

Spend quality time getting to know your defender, Jesus, and make sure you have come to grips with your true identity in Him. The best way to do this is through consistent personal Bible study and prayer. And check and recheck your "battle gear"; make sure each piece is securely in place through daily prayer.

The best way to sum up what I've been trying to say in the pages of this book is this simple truth: The devil is here to take whatever he can. Jesus has come to give us life to the fullest!

In the heat of the spiritual battle, we need to remember who we are—we are soldiers in God's army. And it's our commanding officer, Jesus, who conquered darkness and sin once and for all on the cross. Don't ever forget that this battle sometimes takes all we have, and then some. And as tempting as it is when we get weary to give up in the heat of the struggle, be encouraged that you're not alone. Peter offers this advice: "Stand firm against him, and be strong in your faith. Remember that your Christian brothers and sisters all over the world are going through the same kind of suffering you are. In his kindness God called you to share in his eternal glory by means of Christ Jesus. So after you have suffered a little while, he will restore, support, and strengthen you, and he will place you on a firm foundation" (1 Peter 5:9–10).

So stand up to the devil! Let the Lord use you as a candle in your world, and you'll never regret it!

THINK ABOUT IT

1. What are the three most meaningful things you learned in this book? How do they apply to your daily life?
2. Think of at least one person you know who needs to be rescued from the darkness. Take a few minutes to pray for that person, asking God how He wants to use you to rescue him or her. Then think about what might be the best strategy you can use to reach him or her.
3. List at least three ways or places where God is calling you to be a candle in the darkness right now. What do you need to do? When? With whom? Where?
4. What does it mean to stay close to Jesus? How can you accomplish this in your everyday life?
5. What's going to be the most difficult area in your life to take a stand against the devil? Spend a few minutes in prayer, asking God to help you in this area. Then ask a trusted friend to pray for you and keep you accountable.

Appendix A

Satanic/Occult Symbols

Anarchy. Represents the abolition of all law and the denial of authority. Initially, those into punk music used this symbol. Now it is widely used by the followers of heavy metal music and self-styled Satanists—"do what thou wilt."

Ankh. An ancient Egyptian symbol of life often associated with fertility. The top portion represents the female, and the lower portion symbolizes the male. A spirit of lust is the power of this union of male/female.

Anti-justice. The Roman symbol for justice was an upright double-bladed ax. The representation of anti-justice or rebellion inverts the double-bladed ax.

Baphomet or demon symbol. Unique to Satanism. A demonic deity and symbolic of Satan. Often appears on jewelry.

Black mass indicators. These signs can be used as a source of direction as well as a sign of involvement in black masses. Holy items are defiled and the Lord's Prayer is recited backwards.

Blood ritual. Represents human and animal sacrifices.

 Cross of confusion or satanic cross. Ancient Roman symbol questioning the existence or deity of God. Within the occult it is the representation of the three crown princes: Satan, Belial, and Leviathan. It symbolizes complete power under Lucifer.

 Cross of Nero. Represented peace in the '60s. Another symbol that mocks the cross of Christ. Among heavy metal and occult groups it signifies the defeat of Christianity (an inverted cross with the cross anchor broken downward).

 Diana and Lucifer. The moon goddess Diana and the "son of the morning" Lucifer are found in nearly all types of witchcraft and Satanism. When the moon faces the opposite direction, it is primarily a witchcraft symbol.

 Goat Head. The horned goat, goat of mendes, Baphomet, god of the witches, the scapegoat. It's a Satanist's way of mocking Jesus as the "Lamb" who died for our sins.

 Hexagram. Also referred to as the seal of Solomon, the hexagram is said to be one of the most powerful symbols in the occult. It's used to work magic.

Horned hand. A sign of recognition among those in the occult. When pointed at someone, it is meant to place a curse on that person. Those attending heavy metal concerts also use it to affirm allegiance to the music's message of negativism.

666 FFF **Mark of the beast.** Four different representations of the mark of the beast or Satan. Note the letter F is the sixth letter in the alphabet.

 **Pentagram.** A five-pointed star, with or without the circle, is an important symbol in witchcraft and in most forms of magic. Generally, the top point represents the spirit and the other points represent wind, fire, earth, and water.

 Sample altar. The altar may be any flat object where the implements of the ritual are placed. Usually the altar will be placed within a nine-foot circle. It could be as large as forty-eight inches long, twenty-two inches wide, and two inches high. The pentagram in the center is etched into the slab. Human or animal blood is then poured into the etching. Other symbols may be carved according to individual group traditions. Implements on the altar may include a chalice, candles, parchment, a cauldron, and the Book of Shadows. A smaller version of the altar can be found in the bedrooms, closets, etc., of young self-styled Satanists or dabblers.

Swastika (broken cross). A symbol of ancient origin, sometimes called a Sun Wheel, it originally represented the four winds, the four seasons, and the four points of the compass. At that time its arms were at 90-degree angles turned the opposite direction from what is depicted here. The swastika shown here represents the elements or forces turning against nature and out of harmony. Neo-Nazis and occult groups use it in this manner.

Appendix B

Occult, Satanic, and Witchcraft Terms

Alchemy. Often associated with medieval folklore, this is a chemical science and speculative philosophy designed to transform base metals into gold. It is figuratively used regarding the change of base human nature into the divine.

Altered states. States other than normal waking consciousness, such as daydreaming; sleep-dreaming; hypnotic trance; meditative, mystical, or drug-induced states; or unconscious states.

Black mass. Held in honor of the devil on the witches' Sabbath. The ritual reverses the Roman Catholic mass, desecrating the objects used in worship. Sometimes the participants drink the blood of an animal during the ceremony. Often a nude woman is stretched out on the altar, and the high priest concludes the ritual by having sex with her.

Book of Shadows. Also called a grimoire, this journal is kept either by individual witches or Satanists or by a coven to record the activities of the group and the incantations used.

Chalice. A silver goblet used for blood communion.

Clairaudience. The ability to hear mentally without using the ears.

Clairvoyance. The ability to see mentally beyond ordinary time and space without using the eyes. Also called "second sight."

Coven. A group of Satanists who gather to perform rites. There are traditionally thirteen members, but with self-styled groups the number varies. A coven is also called a clan.

Crystals. Those involved in the occult and witchcraft believe that crystals contain incredible heating and energizing powers. Crystals are often touted as being able to restore the flow of energy in the human body.

Curse. Invocation of an oath associated with black magic or sorcery intended to harm or destroy property or opponents.

Divination. Methods of discovering the personal, human significance of present or future events. The means to obtain insights may include dreams, hunches, involuntary body actions, mediumistic possession, consulting the dead, observing the behavior of animals and birds, tossing coins, casting lots, and reading natural phenomena.

Druids. A branch of dangerous and powerful Celtic priests from pre-Christian Britain and Gaul who are still active today. They worship the sun and believe in the immortality of the soul and reincarnation. They are also skilled in medicine and astronomy.

Esoteric. Used to describe knowledge that is possessed or understood by a select few.

Gnosticism. The secret doctrines and practices of mysticism whereby a person may come to the enlightenment or realization that he is of the same essence as God or the Absolute. The Greek word gnosis means knowledge. At the heart of Gnostic thought is the idea that revelation of the hidden gnosis frees one from the fragmentary and illusory material world and teaches him about the origins of the spiritual world to which the Gnostic belongs by nature.

Initiation. An occult term generally used in reference to the expansion or transformation of a person's consciousness. An initiate is one whose consciousness has been transformed to perceive inner realities. There are varying degrees of initiation, such as first degree, second degree, etc.

Inner self. The inner divine nature possessed by human beings. All people are said to possess an inner self, though they may not be aware of it.

Karma. The debt accumulated against the soul as a result of good or bad actions committed during one's life (or lives). If one accumulates good karma, he supposedly will be reincarnated to a desirable state. If one accumulates bad karma, he will be reincarnated to a less desirable state.

Magick. Magic that employs ritual symbols and ceremony, including ceremonial costumes, dramatic invocations to gods, potent incense, and mystic sacraments.

Magick Circle. A circle inscribed on the floor of a temple for ceremonial purposes. Often nine feet in diameter, it is believed to hold magical powers within and protect those involved in the ceremony from evil.

Magister. The male leader of a coven.

Magus. A male witch.

Mantra. A holy word, phrase, or verse in Hindu or Buddhist meditation techniques. A mantra is usually provided to an initiate by a guru who supposedly holds specific insights regarding the needs of his pupils. The vibrations of the mantra are said to lead the mediator into union with the divine source within.

Monism. Literally means one. In a spiritual framework it refers to the classical occult philosophy that all is one; all reality may be reduced to a single unifying principle partaking of the same essence and reality. Monism also relates to the belief that there is no ultimate distinction between the creator and the creation (pantheism).

Mysticism. The belief that God is totally different from anything the human mind can think and must be approached by a mind without content. Spiritual union or direct communion with ultimate reality can be obtained through subjective experience such as intuition or a unifying vision.

Necromancy. A practice in which the spirits of the dead are summoned to provide omens for discovering secrets of past or future events.

Necrophilia. An act of sexual intercourse with a corpse.

Neo-Paganism. A loosely defined system of worshiping nature and the gods of nature.

Nirvana. Literally a blowing out or cooling of the fires of existence. It is the main term in Buddhism for the final release from the cycle of birth and death into bliss.

Numerology. The analysis of hidden prophetic meanings of numbers.

Occult. From the Latin *occultus*, meaning "secret" or "hidden." The occult refers to secret or hidden knowledge available to initiates, to the supernatural, and sometimes to paranormal phenomena and parapsychology. Occultists believe in things like astrology, alchemy, and divination to help them bring about whatever effects they desire.

Pagan. From the Latin word *paganus*, meaning country dwellers. "Pagans" were country folk who clung to the old rural religions of Nature worship.

Pantheism. The belief that God and the world are ultimately identical; all is God. Everything that exists constitutes a unity, and this all-inclusive unity is divine. God is equated with the forces and laws of the universe but is not a personal being.

Poltergeist. German word for a noisy, mischievous, destructive spirit (demon).

Psychic. A medium, "sensitive," or channeler. Also refers to paranormal events that can't be explained by established physical principles.

Psychic birth. A quickening of spiritual or cosmic consciousness and power. This new consciousness recognizes oneness with God and the universe. Psychic birth is an occult counterpart to the Christian new birth.

Psychokinesis (PK). The power of the mind to influence matter or move objects (see also *telekinesis*).

Reincarnation. The belief that the soul moves from one bodily existence to another until, usually after many lives, it is released from historical existence and absorbed into the Absolute.

Ritual. A prescribed form of religious or magical ceremony.

Runes. A northern European alphabet used by occult groups in secret writing. There are several forms of runes.

Santeria. A mingling of African tribal religions and Catholicism, established by African slaves brought to the Americas and the Caribbean.

Séance. A gathering of people seeking communication with deceased loved ones or famous historical figures through a medium.

Self-realization. A synonym for God-realization. It refers to a personal recognition of one's divinity.

Shaman. A medicine man or witch doctor.

"So mote it be." Words spoken at the end of an occult ceremony. Similar to "amen" in traditional religious services.

Spirit guide. A spiritual entity that provides information or guidance often through a medium or channeler. The spirit provides guidance only after the channeler relinquishes his perceptual and cognitive capacities into its control.

Spiritism. Seeking guidance from dead persons contacted through mediums.

Syncretism. The fusion of different forms of belief or practice; the claim that all religions are one and share the same core teachings.

Talisman. A power object, usually an amulet or trinket.

Telekinesis. A form of psychokinesis (PK); the apparent movement of stationary objects without the use of known physical force.

Third eye. An imaginary eye in the forehead believed to be the center of psychic vision.

Trance. An altered state of consciousness, induced or spontaneous, that gives access to many ordinarily inhibited capacities of the mind-body system. Trance states are generally self-induced.

Visualization. Also known as guided imagery or mind over matter. Visualization is the attempt to bring about change in the material realm by the power of the mind.

Voodoo. An ancient religion combining ancestor worship, sorcery, charms, and spells. Those involved are extremely superstitious and use strange objects to worship.

Warlock. Often used for a male witch, but it actually designates a traitor.

Wicca. Gets its root from the Anglo-Saxon word *wicca*. It means to shape or bend nature to your advantage.

Witch. A male or female practitioner of any sort of witchcraft.

Witchcraft. Known as the "Old Religion," it is an ancient practice dating back to biblical times. It is defined as the performance of magic forbidden by God for non-biblical ends. The word *witchcraft* is related to the Old English word *wicca,* the practice of magical arts, occultic arts, and nature worship.

Zen. A type of Buddhism known for its emphasis on breaking down the commitment and attachment to the logical and rational ordering of experience.

Zodiac. The imaginary belt in the heavens that encompasses the apparent paths of the principal planets except Pluto. Divided into twelve constellations or signs based on the assumed dates that the sun enters each of these "houses" or symbols, the zodiac is used for predictions in astrology.

APPENDIX C

SATANIC HOLIDAYS

January 17. Satanic and demon revels.

January 31. Imbolc or Candlemas. Day of indulgence and fertility.

February 2. Satanic and demon revels.

March 21. The spring equinox, Satanist New Year, or Crux.

April 30. Beltane or Walpurgisnacht, day of lust and indulgence.

June 21. The summer solstice, day of celebrating one's sense of humor.

July 1. Satanic and demon revels.

July 31. Lughnasadh, day of celebration of being the predator, not the prey.

August 3. Satanic and demon revels.

August 24. Fundus Mundi.

September 7. Marriage to the Beast.

September 21. The autumn equinox, time to reflect on oneself.

October 31. Halloween or Samhain. The Fire Festival, the time to settle the score with destruction rituals, curses, and revenge.

December 21. The winter solstice. Celebration of being self-emancipated.

December 24. Satanic sacrificial ritual, demon revels, and Grand High Climax.

Your birthday. Celebration of your birth and a celebration of life and your accomplishments. One of the highest ritual holidays.

Friday the thirteenth. All of these days are satanic holidays.

Full moon. All full moon nights provide reason for major occult activity.

notes

Chapter 2
1. *ABC News 20/20,* December 4, 1992.

Chapter 3
1. David Kinnaman, *Ministry to Mosaics: Teens and the Supernatural* (Ventura, CA: The Barna Group, 2006), 25.
2. *www.heavensgate.com.*

Chapter 4
1. Carl M. Cannon, "Honey, I Warped the Kids," *Motherjones,* July/August 1993, 19.
2. Ibid., 20.
3. George Barna, *Real Teens* (Ventura, CA: Regal Books, 2001), 93.
4. George Barna, *Teens and the Supernatural* (Ventura, CA: Regal Books, 2002).
5. Barna, *Real Teens,* 26.
6. Ibid.

Chapter 5
1. Steven Levy, "The Low Cost of Guitar Heroism," *Newsweek,* January 29, 2007, 24.
2. Barna, *Real Teens,* 73.
3. Ibid., 26.
4. Ibid., 29.
5. *www.eminem.com.*
6. Dan Epstein, *Revolver,* September/October 2001, 86.
7. Anthony DeCurtis, "Marilyn Manson: The Beliefnet Interview," *www.beliefnet.com/story/78/story_7870_1.html.*
8. U.S. Census Bureau: Teenage Research Unlimited, Fall 1998; Nielsen 2Q '99, Youth Markets Alert April 1998 and Dubrow "Advertising Recognition Recall by Age," 1995, Nielsen Media Research, 3Q'01.
9. Jessica Kovler, "Researcher confirms existence of 'earworms,'" *San Francisco Chronicle,* August 12, 2003, A-2.

Chapter 6

1. *http://lindenlab.com/employment*.
2. *PC Gamer,* May 2003, 50–51.

Chapter 7

1. *www.LaurieCabot.com*.
2. "Witchcraft Is a Religion," *Sassy,* March 1992, 64–65, 80–81.
3. *www.hecatescauldron.org*.
4. Silver Ravenwolf, *Teen Witch* (St. Paul: Llewellyn Publications, 2000), 5–8.
5. Scott Cunningham, *The Truth About Witchcraft* (St. Paul: Llewellyn Publications, 1997), 72.
6. Ibid., 75.
7. Michele Morgan, *Simple Wicca* (Berkeley: Conari Press, 2000), 8.
8. Craig S. Hawkins, *Goddess Worship, Witchcraft, and Neo-Paganism* (Grand Rapids: Zondervan, 1998), 8–11.
9. Ibid., 44.
10. Jamie Wood, *The Teen Spell Book* (Berkeley: Celestial Arts, 2001).
11. Al Menconi, *The Hot 200* (New Song Publishing, 1987), 7.

Chapter 8

1. Otto Friedrich, "New Age Harmonies," *www.time.com/time/magazine/article/0,9171,966129=1,00.html*.
2. David Kinnaman, *The Barna Group,* 2006, 6–7.
3. Roy Rivenburg, "Golf with Deepak," *Los Angeles Times,* May 3, 2003, E10.
4. *www.religion-cults.com*.

Chapter 9

1. Gallup News Service, "Americans' Belief in Psychic and Paranormal Phenomena Is Up over Last Decade," Frank Newport and Maura Strausberg, Princeton, NJ, June 8, 2001.
2. Ron Rhodes, *Angels Among Us* (Eugene, OR: Harvest House, 1994), 29–34.
3. Billy Graham, *Angels: God's Secret Agents* (New York: Doubleday, 1975), 2–3.
4. Ibid., 3–4.

Chapter 10
1. *www.freedominion.ca/phpBB2/rss.php?t=32147.*

Chapter 11
1. Henry Parry Liddon, *Liddon's Bampton Lectures, 1866* (London: Rivingtons, 1869), 148, quoted in Ravi Zacharias, *Jesus Among Other Gods* (Nashville: W Publishing Group, 2000).

Chapter 12
1. Keith Wegeman, *Guideposts*, February 1958, reprinted at *www.jesus.beliefnet.com/story/99/story_9954.html.*

Chapter 14
1. George Barna, *Real Teens* (Oxnard, CA: Regal Books, 2001), 125, 133.

Chapter 16
1. Chuck Colson, *The Body* (Dallas, TX: Word Publishing, 1992), 58–61.

CONTACT INFORMATION

For more information on other resources, radio and TV shows, *Real Answers* evangelistic events, and "Choices" school assemblies, please contact:

Real Answers with Steve Russo
P.O. Box 1549
Ontario, California 91762
(909) 466-7060
FAX (909) 466-7056

E-mail: Russoteam@realanswers.com

You can also visit our Web sites at:
www.realanswers.com